Set design by Michael Yeargan

Photo by T. Charles Erickson

The set of the McCarter Theatre production of *Ridiculous Fraud*.

RIDICULOUS FRAUD

BY BETH HENLEY

DRAMATISTS
PLAY SERVICE
INC.

RIDICULOUS FRAUD
Copyright © 2007, Beth Henley

All Rights Reserved

For Lydy Becker Caldwell

RIDICULOUS FRAUD was originally produced at the McCarter Theatre Center in Princeton, New Jersey, opening on May 12, 2006. It was directed by Lisa Peterson; the set design was by Michael Yeargan; the costume design was by Jess Goldstein; the lighting design was by Peter Kaczorowski; the sound design was by Martin Desjardins; the dramaturg was Janice Paran; the dialect coach was Gillian Lane-Plescia; and the fight consultant was Rick Sordelet. The cast was as follows:

LAFCAD CLAY .... Daniel London
ANDREW CLAY .... Reg Rogers
WILLOW CLAY .... Ali Marsh
KAP CLAY .... Tim DeKay
UNCLE BAITES .... Charles Haid
GEORGIA .... Heather Goldenhersh
MAUDE CHRYSTAL .... Barbara Garrick
ED CHRYSTAL .... John Carroll Lynch

RIDICULOUS FRAUD was subsequently produced by South Coast Repertory (Linda and Tod White, Honorary Producers) in Costa Mesa, California, opening on October 13, 2006. It was directed by Sharon Ott; the set design was by Hugh Landwehr; the costume design was by Joyce Kim Lee; the lighting design was by Peter Maradudin; the sound design was by Stephen LeGrand; the fight director was Martin Noyes; and the dramaturg was John Glore. The cast was as follows:

LAFCAD CLAY .... Ian Fraser
ANDREW CLAY .... Matt McGrath
WILLOW CLAY .... Betsy Brandt
KAP CLAY .... Matt Letscher
UNCLE BAITES .... Randy Oglesby
GEORGIA .... Eliza Pryor
MAUDE CHRYSTAL .... Nike Doukas
ED CHRYSTAL .... Paul Vincent O'Connor

CHARACTERS

LAFCAD CLAY — the youngest brother

ANDREW CLAY — the oldest brother

WILLOW CLAY — Andrew's wife, Ed's daughter

KAP CLAY — the middle brother

BAITES — the boys' uncle

GEORGIA — a lost girl

MAUDE CHRYSTAL — married to Ed

ED CHRYSTAL — Willow's father, Maude's husband

PLACE

Act One, Scene 1: Clay family home in New Orleans, the Garden District. Summer.

Act One, Scene 2: Outside Uncle Baites' farmhouse in the Louisiana backwoods. The following autumn.

Act Two, Scene 1: Kap's cabin and backyard, deep in the woods. The following winter.

Act Two, Scene 2: New Orleans cemetery, the Clay family tomb. The following spring.

TIME

Five years before Hurricane Katrina.

RIDICULOUS FRAUD

ACT ONE

Scene 1

Time: around midnight. New Orleans; Garden District. A stormy summer night. An opulent home, now going to seed. The living room opens onto an overgrown garden. The phone is ringing. Lafcad, a young man dressed in a suit and tie, sits on a velvet sofa hunched over; elbows on knees, hands on head. A ray of lightning. Crash of thunder. Sound of laughter from the entrance hall. The phone stops ringing. Lafcad gets up and goes to hide in the garden. Andrew, Willow, and Kap enter in high spirits.

ANDREW. Lafcad is ridiculous.

WILLOW. He wouldn't dance with me. "No, I'm not dancing. I never dance." He wouldn't dance. Not even with his bride.

ANDREW. He's really … it's ridiculous. He really can dance. Mother gave him lessons. Waltzes, tangos, tap … He jitterbugs.

WILLOW. *(To Kap.)* Kap dance. Boogie dance. *(Kap and Willow boogie dance. Andrew makes drinks.)* Boogie; boogie! *(Kap whistles.)*

ANDREW. It's going to rain.

WILLOW. I love the rain. A summer rain. *(Kap whistles in agreement. The dancing stops.)* Lafcad did look happy.

KAP. I didn't notice that he did. *(Andrew hands Willow a drink.)*

ANDREW. He's not a people person. There's an effort. His toast was imperfect.

WILLOW. He didn't mention his bride.

ANDREW. Egregious oversight. *(To Willow.)* I mentioned you.

My lovely wife.

WILLOW. Yes.

KAP. You mentioned everyone.

ANDREW. What? Was my toast too long? It takes time to create a mood. The bride's mother came up to me after and promised to vote for me for State Auditor. The father said nothing. He has that money-stunted glare. Ah! I went on too long. About the past. About the future. Children; grandchildren; great-grandchildren. I used the word progeny.

KAP. Twice.

ANDREW. *(To Kap.)* But you didn't say anything. You didn't even toast.

KAP. I did.

WILLOW. He said, "Cheers!"

KAP. I meant it.

WILLOW. I have to change my feet.

KAP. Your pretty feet. *(Willow exits.)*

ANDREW. It's easy to be taciturn. But Lafcad's our brother. Daddy couldn't be there. I wanted to take up the slack. Did anyone say anything to you about him? Our father?

KAP. I got some solid shoulder pats. A couple of brave winks.

ANDREW. He sent a letter. He gave me a letter to read at the dinner. He gave it to me when I went to visit. It's here in my pocket.

KAP. You didn't read it? You kept it in your pocket?

ANDREW. I don't think Lafcad would have appreciated me pointing out the fact that our father is incarcerated in the penitentiary and I really didn't think the letter was well-written. I found it riddled with clichés, sentimentality, self-aggrandizements. What are you thinking? Are you thinking I've made a mistake?

KAP. Yeah.

ANDREW. Okay. Well, there's one opinion. I go to visit him more than you. That's why he gave me the letter. I'm the one who's out there being encouraging.

KAP. Who was the girl in the gold dress?

ANDREW. Teresa Gilroy. She's married to one of my potential contributors; don't try to snatch her up. I know how you do that but she's taken. Totally taken. Don't pursue.

KAP. I'm not doing much 'til duck season.

ANDREW. Get a wife! You need a wife! After tomorrow you'll be the only one of us who isn't married. Lafcad is younger than you and he'll be married. It's like you're unfortunately becoming one of those Peter Pan types. Quaint waterfowl guide to wealthy NRA old-timers and it's starting to wear thin.

KAP. There's one opinion.

ANDREW. You're squandering all of your prodigious potential. If Mama were alive she'd be heartsick. I'm telling you this because our father is not in a position to, and you need some guidance. *(The following exchange between Kap and Andrew is playful but there is an undercurrent.)*

KAP. You're telling me this, Andrew, because you're an asshole.

ANDREW. I try to open up …

KAP. Please don't.

ANDREW. Fine. Play the redneck-bubba.

KAP. I'd like to punch your face.

ANDREW. Don't try it.

KAP. I could take you.

ANDREW. Don't try it, little brother.

KAP. Yeah. I could though. *(Willow enters dancing in bedroom slippers.)*

WILLOW. *(About her feet.)* "Free at last, free at last! Thank God Almighty we're free at last."

KAP. Her dancing feet.

ANDREW. I wonder where Uncle Baites and Georgia are?

KAP. Hobbling home.

ANDREW. Shut up, Kap.

KAP. She has a wooden leg. She hobbles; it's reality. *(Kap exits.)*

ANDREW. Kap's jealous. I think he feels left behind. He doesn't have a real job; he's not married. Everyone's growing up and he's being left behind. Why do you take up for him?

WILLOW. I don't.

ANDREW. Do you think this is a good thing? Me running for State Auditor?

WILLOW. I do.

ANDREW. The press has been heartlessly biased against Daddy and it is incumbent upon me to bolster the family name. I can, you know. I'm a genuinely honest man.

WILLOW. You are. You are.

ANDREW. It's a rare thing, honesty. Sadly it's so. *(Uncle Baites, fifties, and Georgia, a young girl with a limp, enter.)*

UNCLE BAITES. Hello! We're here.

9

WILLOW. Uncle Baites, come in. Hello, Georgia, have a seat.

GEORGIA. Thanks.

ANDREW. Great night, huh? I teared up more than once. More than once.

WILLOW. *(To Baites.)* Lovely poem you read. Did you write it?

UNCLE BAITES. For the occasion.

WILLOW. It moved me. Really, really.

GEORGIA. When you read it, you shook. Why were you shaking so hard?

UNCLE BAITES. Because I don't like weddings. They unnerve me.

WILLOW. You don't like weddings?

UNCLE BAITES. Not at all.

ANDREW. It wasn't even the real wedding. What will you do tomorrow at the real wedding, I wonder?

GEORGIA. *(To Andrew.)* Your speech was too long.

ANDREW. What?

GEORGIA. I got so tired when you were talking. Everyone did.

ANDREW. Really? Not really?

GEORGIA. People were yawning all over the room.

WILLOW. Georgia, how long have you and Uncle Baites been friends?

GEORGIA. Not long.

UNCLE BAITES. No, not long.

GEORGIA. We met today. This morning at the train station. I asked him for some change and he invited me to the wedding. He got me this dress. *(The phone rings.)*

UNCLE BAITES. It's true. What have you got to drink? *(The phone rings.)* She likes red cherries with bourbon. *(Kap enters with the phone.)*

KAP. Willow, baby, your daddy is calling you!

WILLOW. Ugh! Oh, ugh! *(Willow takes the phone upstage. Andrew goes to the bar. Baites follows him. The following exchange between Baites and Andrew is meant to be private.)*

ANDREW. Uncle Baites, I don't think this is smart. I don't think this girl is a good idea.

UNCLE BAITES. Please, I'm an old man. What do I know.

ANDREW. It's dangerous picking up a stranger.

UNCLE BAITES. I want to get her a better leg. A lightweight one she can run on.

ANDREW. I'm telling you, she could be some sort of swindler.

UNCLE BAITES. Oh, I don't care about that. *(Willow sets down the phone.)*

WILLOW. You won't believe this! It's unbelievable! The whole wedding is off.

ANDREW. No, that's impossible! What do you mean?!

WILLOW. Right after the dinner Lafcad broke off the engagement to Mary Anna! She said that he tore her dress!

UNCLE BAITES. *(Overlapping from "engagement.")* When did this occur? Where is he now?

KAP. *(Overlapping from "occur.")* Why did he tear it? What did she do?

ANDREW. *(Overlapping from "tear it.")* He wouldn't tear a dress. This is crazy!

UNCLE BAITES. Where is he now?

WILLOW. I don't know anything. It's likely they have it all wrong.

ANDREW. There's no question they do.

WILLOW. Daddy drinks and tells lies.

ANDREW. Yes, he's gotten it all wrong! Certainly because it is an absurd notion. The tearing … it's ridiculous. Georgia, here is your drink.

UNCLE BAITES. They don't have the cherries. No garnishes. Oh my God, I hope this isn't all my fault.

ANDREW. Oh really, Uncle Baites, what in the world…?

UNCLE BAITES. History repeats itself.

ANDREW. What?

UNCLE BAITES. Genetics plays a part and I have some bad marital genes that he could have inherited.

ANDREW. What are you talking about? What does he mean?

UNCLE BAITES. My engagement. I was engaged to Beatrice Slater. This was years ago. A benchmark in my life. I can't tell you why I did not drive to the church that day. I put on my tuxedo and got into my Pontiac. I stopped at the gas station to fill it up and drove. A long way. I have endured years of loneliness since and all I dream of is love.

ANDREW. There's no such thing as what you are talking about. Marital genes. It's a fiction.

UNCLE BAITES. Yes. I'm sure. I'm sure. *(Baites goes out and stands in the garden. Lafcad conceals himself from Baites.)*

ANDREW. I'm definite about this. Lafcad has to get married tomorrow. Our family cannot suffer another humiliating blow.

KAP. No. Not really.

ANDREW. What do you mean?

KAP. I'm agreeing with you.

ANDREW. Why are you smirking?

KAP. I must be amused. *(The doorbell rings.)*

WILLOW. It's them! Daddy and that awful woman!

ANDREW. They're coming here now?

WILLOW. I won't greet her. He exalted that horrible woman. All night he called her, "his wife." My mother's not dead six months! I can't do it. *(Willow exits.)*

ANDREW. Ed shouldn't have married so quickly. His wife was hardly dead. Barely in her grave.

KAP. I'll get it. I like the new stepmother. *(Kap exits to the entrance hall. Georgia and Andrew wait a moment. Sudden flash of lightning. Roll of thunder.)*

ANDREW. So, Georgia, are you enjoying the festivities?

GEORGIA. Yeah.

ANDREW. And what happened to your leg?

GEORGIA. That's personal.

ANDREW. Yes, of course.

GEORGIA. I don't like you pointing out my body parts.

ANDREW. Please, forgive me. A tasteless remark. Uncharacteristic indeed. You see, I'm trying, I must hold this family together all by myself without glue. There's no glue. Just blood. No paste. *(Flash of lightning; thunder. Kap enters with Maude Chrystal, forties, a terrifically striking woman.)*

KAP. Andy, your stepmother-in-law has arrived.

ANDREW. Maude, welcome, welcome.

KAP. Georgia, you've met Maude Chrystal.

MAUDE. Hello, Georgia.

GEORGIA. Hi.

ANDREW. Where's Ed?

MAUDE. Parking.

ANDREW. Tell us what happened. There's been some mistake.

MAUDE. Lafcad broke the engagement.

ANDREW. But he wouldn't. He couldn't. The wedding's tomorrow.

MAUDE. May I smoke?

KAP. Of course.

ANDREW. Outside, please. In the garden. We're having to sell Daddy's house. Our family home. It's on the market. It's listed.

Everyone knows that. Everyone knows all about our desperation.

MAUDE. Yes. *(Maude goes into the garden. Kap starts to follow but Georgia calls to him.)*

GEORGIA. Hey, Kap.

KAP. Yeah?

GEORGIA. This new dress itches me. Where can I change? *(Kap helps Georgia get up.)*

KAP. This way.

GEORGIA. I've been scratching myself.

KAP. Really? I've missed it. Show me where. *(Georgia smiles and shoves him.)*

GEORGIA. Ah, you ain't so much.

KAP. Nothing at all. *(They exit. Andrew freshens his drink. In the garden Maude walks over to Baites.)*

MAUDE. Hello, Baites.

UNCLE BAITES. Maude.

MAUDE. Cigarette?

UNCLE BAITES. No, no. I've become too old to hang myself.

MAUDE. Ridiculous. Have a smoke.

UNCLE BAITES. No, no. *(Lafcad appears.)*

LAFCAD. I'd like a Coke.

UNCLE BAITES. Lafcad! What are you doing?

LAFCAD. Shh. Don't tell anyone. You must not. They are going to give me such grief. Please, mention me to no one.

MAUDE. No.

LAFCAD. Uncle Baites, could you see if you could find me a Coke and some sort of food? I need to fuel myself for battle. I ate nothing at the dinner. Nothing.

UNCLE BAITES. Alright.

LAFCAD. I'm sure I don't deserve food. It's all monstrous. I'm monstrous.

UNCLE BAITES. Please. There's nothing you can do. It's genetics. *(Uncle Baites goes into the living room. Andrew is dialing the phone. Baites hears some of the call as he exits.)*

ANDREW. *(Into phone.)* Lafcad, where are you? What happened? What have you done? Call me as soon as you get this call because this is a catastrophe and it's rude as hell, okay?! Call me. *(Lafcad gives Maude a look. They have both heard the call.)*

LAFCAD. Excuse me, I have to hide. *(Lafcad hides. Kap enters the living room.)*

ANDREW. *(To Kap.)* He's not at his apartment. I called him and he's not there.

KAP. Oh.

ANDREW. What do you think happened?

KAP. Who knows.

ANDREW. It's too late to renege. People have come from out of town. Airfares have been paid, non-refundable airfares and mileage points!

KAP. Yeah. It's messy.

ANDREW. Oh, Kap, Kap. What's wrong with our brother?

KAP. He's always been strange.

ANDREW. Yeah.

KAP. Remember how he couldn't stand to watch people eat scrambled eggs?

ANDREW. Mama had to give up serving eggs entirely.

KAP. And how he'd pull your nose to make certain it was really your face and not a masked imposter. He'd have to pull it really hard.

ANDREW. Mama never should have given him dance lessons. She should have just backed off. I'm probably way off base here but I mean Lafcad … could have tendencies and that's okay. As long as he gets married tomorrow, let the chips fall where they may.

KAP. You think Lafcad has … what?

ANDREW. He didn't take a date to his prom.

KAP. That wasn't because … it wasn't "tendencies." He just couldn't get a date. No one he asked would go. He wasn't popular.

ANDREW. What? He wasn't popular? Really? You and I were both popular. I never realized Lafcad was not. Oh, that makes me so sad. Still it's all okay as long as tomorrow he gets married to Mary Anna Lancaster. She's really, really rich and Lafcad will have a big chance for happiness. God, all the money that's been spent. That dinner tonight. Dinner at Antoine's for thirty-two people. Don't worry, Kap, I'll pay you back.

KAP. For what?

ANDREW. The check; you picked up the check.

KAP. No.

ANDREW. Yes, I insist. You can't afford all that. I want to participate.

KAP. You did. I paid with your card. Willow gave it to me.

ANDREW. Does this mean … I thought … I'm to pay for the

14

whole event?

KAP. The problem is, Andrew, no one else has any money.

ANDREW. I don't have money.

KAP. Take it out of what's made from selling this place.

ANDREW. All that goes to Daddy's lawyers and creditors; retribution payments. Daddy has nothing. I have to send him money for the prison canteen. Oh God, how much was it? The bill? How much?

KAP. Steep.

ANDREW. How much? Over one thousand? Over two thousand? Over how much?

KAP. There was tip. I'm a generous tipper.

ANDREW. I'm not about making money. I want to serve people. I'm not about making a killing.

KAP. Get it from Willow.

ANDREW. She's not a bank! She's my wife. I won't do that. Let me see that receipt. Where's the receipt?

KAP. I don't know. I just signed it. I didn't take a receipt.

ANDREW. You didn't take a receipt? Grow up, Kap, please! Because this is — you're not a kid. We have to be responsible! It's not going to help Daddy's appeal if we're out there perpetrating things: not paying our debts, not taking receipts! *(The doorbell rings.)* That's Ed. *(Andrew exits to the front door. Kap goes out on the balcony.)*

KAP. Hello, Mrs. Chrystal. I believe your husband's arrived.

MAUDE. Smoke?

KAP. No thanks. But I like to watch. You mind?

MAUDE. I don't. *(Kap watches Maude smoke. Andrew and Ed Chrystal enter.)*

ED. It's a mess! A fucking mess! The Lancasters have staked out Lafcad's apartment. The girl may sue: wedding costs, emotional damages, fraud.

ANDREW. I can't let this happen; it won't happen.

ED. Where's Willow? She was acting like a tuke all night.

ANDREW. I think she's resting.

ED. She can't rest! This is a family crisis. Go get her. Go on. Just get me my daughter! *(Andrew exits. Maude and Kap come in from the garden. Spotting Maude:)* There you are!

MAUDE. I am.

ED. Couldn't find a place to park. New Orleans is a terrible town.

I can't wait to get back to Covington where it's clean! *(To Kap.)* Your brother is a pissant shit, you know that?

KAP. No.

ED. You gonna take me duck hunting this season? Mallards, blue teal. I hear you got some secret honey holes. I'll rent you out and your dog. What's the charge?

KAP. Just money.

ED. And I bag the limit?

KAP. Nothing's certain. Weather conditions change. Water conditions change. Ducks are highly mobile. They got wings and they're highly mobile.

ED. I like the deer. They stay right where they are on my property. I gotta get you over to the deer camp. Got us a gourmet cook. You ever hunt deer? I mean besides the two-legged kind?

KAP. No.

ED. Why not?

KAP. Shooting deer be kinda like shooting my dog. Those big ole eyes. Couldn't do it.

ED. But you shoot the duck.

KAP. Yeah.

ED. They're harder to shoot. A smaller animal. Reptilian. I hear you hit 'em in the head every time. What's up with your brother?

KAP. Don't know.

ED. Gotta find him before they do. People want to hurt him because it's ugly. *(Baites enters with a sandwich and Coke.)* Lynch. I heard the word lynch. Baites, you know where Lafcad is? You heard from him since dinner?

UNCLE BAITES. No.

ED. Tar and feather. Lynch.

KAP. Drinks?

MAUDE. Sure.

ED. *(To Baites.)* You still hungry?

UNCLE BAITES. Yes.

ED. I'm stuffed. Filled up on Bienville. Feels like rain. Radio station said it was gonna storm. I can smell the water. Feel the stillness.

KAP. *(Giving Ed a drink.)* Scotch.

ED. How'd you know?

KAP. Your wife.

ED. She knows me. She knows me. *(To Baites.)* Why aren't you eating?

UNCLE BAITES. I am. I'm eating. *(He takes a small bite of the sandwich.)*

ED. Who was that crippled kid you were with?

UNCLE BAITES. A friend. Georgia.

ED. Georgia who?

UNCLE BAITES. I'm not sure. I don't know. I used to know things. There was a time I felt I had something of value to impart: I spoke; I lectured; I taught classes on "The Beast Spectacles of Ancient Rome." Now I've forgotten or don't want to know. Why is everyone suddenly so inquisitive?! Excuse me, I'm going ... I prefer to eat in the garden. *(Baites goes into the garden and disappears.)*

ED. It's going to pour. The humidity. He reminds me of your mama. Same strange temperament.

KAP. What?

ED. They were twins. Baites and your mama was twins.

KAP. Yeah, I know that.

ED. Not identical; similar. Your mama was wild. She and your daddy — Madeline and Aidan — were on the party. When they danced together it was something else ... I got a duck call for my birthday. Willow gave it to me. She wants me to take up duck hunting. She thinks it's a more gentlemanly hunt; different echelon sort of hunt. The elite sport. What do you think?

KAP. It's a sickness. More scotch?

ED. No. *(Andrew enters.)*

ANDREW. Ed, Willow's not feeling well.

ED. Where is she?

ANDREW. I'm sorry, Ed; she's really —

ED. I know my own daughter. She needs to see me. Willow, where are you?! Willow?!

WILLOW. *(Offstage.)* Daddy!?

ED. Willow!?

WILLOW. *(Offstage.)* I don't want to be bothered! I'm cleaning the shelves!

ED. What shelves?!

WILLOW. *(Offstage.)* In the pantry! *(Ed exits to the pantry.)*

MAUDE. Willow hates me.

ANDREW. No. No.

MAUDE. She'll never like me. I have some good news for her. Something to cheer her up.

ANDREW. What's that?

MAUDE. It seems I'm leaving.

ANDREW. You mean Louisiana?

MAUDE. Don't tell Ed. I haven't broken Doctor's news.

KAP. What news?

MAUDE. Don't listen to me. I've no idea what I'm saying tonight. Really, I'm out of my mind! Please, freshen my drink. *(Georgia enters in her street clothes. Kap pours Maude another drink.)*

GEORGIA. Where's Baites?

ANDREW. In the garden. *(Georgia limps slowly toward the garden.)* Please, I'll get him. I'll find him. I'll get him. Uncle Baites! *(Andrew goes into the garden and disappears.)*

GEORGIA. *(A beat.)* I want to ask him is there still a wedding?

ANDREW. *(Offstage.)* You coward! You false person you! He's hiding; he's hiding.

LAFCAD. *(Overlapping, offstage.)* Ah! Ooh! My sandwich! *(Andrew drags Lafcad onto the stage. Baites follows.)*

ANDREW. He's here all along!

LAFCAD. *(Holding a sandwich.)* I'm eating. I'm eating! I haven't finished my meal! *(Maude sits down and, without looking in a mirror, puts lipstick on her lips.)*

ANDREW. Do you know what you've done?! Do you have any idea of the trouble you've caused? The heartbreak? The worry? The dinner bill; the shame! You've destroyed your life! Your last hope of a legitimate life.

KAP. Andy, come on.

ANDREW. Me come on?! He tore Mary Anna's dress!

LAFCAD. I didn't! I swear! I grabbed her to stop her! She ran; the dress tore; it was torn. I was trying to stop her.

ANDREW. You were trying to stop her! Call her! Baites, the phone. *(Baites goes to get the phone.)* Tell her you had the wedding jitters. A very bad case of wedding nerves. *(Baites brings the phone.)* Tell her, "I love you, Mary Anna, and without you I will perish."

LAFCAD. But I don't want to get married. I don't want Mary Anna. I don't love her. I don't.

ANDREW. Oh God, God, God. What's wrong with him? What's wrong? Why don't you love her? You should love her. She has so many qualities I admire.

LAFCAD. I do. I admire her too. If only I hadn't misjudged. Help me, Uncle Baites. I don't want to get married. I misjudged. I misjudged.

UNCLE BAITES. It will all be fine. Eventually you'll see.

ANDREW. Why?! Why are you doing this now?!

LAFCAD. I only realized tonight; in the men's room. There must have been signs. All along I ignored. I wanted to change my life. I hate my life and I wanted it to be rosy. I thought this was the way. But tonight in the men's room, standing at the porcelain sink, squirting out the soap, spreading pink foam over my hands, I thought — video — I must stop the recording of the videotape. I hurried out and I found her, Mary Anna, standing by the door laughing and hugging people goodbye. I took her by the arm. I had pink soap on my hands and it smeared on her bare arm and she said, "Wait, my bag!" But I didn't wait: I pulled her out the door and down the street, 'round the corner, under an awning. I stopped. I told her, "My darling, please, we cannot have those people videotaping our wedding. All this documentation will devour the true moment of our being!" I can't believe her response. "It's digital," she said, "It's a digital camera, not video." I told her we were very lucky that we had discovered in the nick of time what an egregious error it would be to live out our infinitesimal lives as one. Please, I told her, keep my mother's ring and godspeed. She did not take it well. She had some points. The truth hurts. It hurts.

ANDREW. You little brat.

LAFCAD. Fine. But Daddy would be proud that I found the courage to be honest and true.

ANDREW. Daddy is in jail for fraud.

LAFCAD. It was a miscarriage of justice and we all believe that! We — all of us do!

ANDREW. Yes, of course we do, we do. He is ... He was ...

LAFCAD. One of the reasons ... I thought if I got married they would relent and let him out to come to his youngest son's wedding.

KAP. Lafcad.

LAFCAD. We could all be together again dressed in tuxedoes, eating cake.

KAP. That's fucking pitiful.

LAFCAD. I was wondering what you thought of all this. I'm going home.

KAP. Don't go home! There are people waiting there for you.

LAFCAD. But why?

ANDREW. You have to realize there are consequences! You can't just do horrible things like this and not think people will want retribution. Because they will; they do.

LAFCAD. What do they want?

KAP. They want to clobber you.

ANDREW. And sue. They want to sue.

LAFCAD. I'm so sorry about all this. Oh God, I don't want to be hit in the face. Where can I go? I can't stay here. Where can I go?

UNCLE BAITES. Come home with me to the backwoods. No one ever comes there.

LAFCAD. Yes, alright. Take me now. I'd better go now.

UNCLE BAITES. I have to pack.

LAFCAD. Yes, then do.

GEORGIA. Am I going?

UNCLE BAITES. You're invited. Your company is requested.

GEORGIA. *(A beat.)* Yeah. I'll go.

LAFCAD. Hurry, please, they may come here looking for me. *(Baites and Georgia exit. The three brothers stand in silence for a moment.)* I know what you think of me, sneaking off into the night. I hear the cacophony in both your heads. *(Lafcad disappears into the garden.)*

ANDREW. I just want to kill him.

KAP. I know.

ANDREW. Maybe I should have given him Daddy's letter. If the letter had been read …

WILLOW. *(Offstage.)* No, Daddy, I won't! I won't ever be civil to that woman! I won't! *(Offstage sound of a jar breaking.)*

KAP. *(To Maude.)* How are you?

MAUDE. Enjoying myself.

KAP. It's amusing, yeah. *(Ed enters, distraught.)*

ED. What's going on? Anyone heard from Lafcad?

KAP. The wedding's off, Ed.

ED. That's not really helpful for anyone. No one. Your family is ruined and mine is tainted. Have you spoken to the Lancasters?

ANDREW. Not yet.

ED. Make that call. I've had enough. My daughter's a handful. I don't know where she gets her stuff. She's not speaking to me except to spit vitriol and bullshit. *(To Maude.)* Let's go, darling, you were right. No sense in trying. A waste of breath. Let's go.

MAUDE. Good night.

ANDREW. Yes, good night.

KAP. 'Bye. *(Ed and Maude exit.)*

ANDREW. *(About Lafcad.)* Is Lafcad out there? Can you see him?

KAP. *(Spying out in the garden.)* Yeah.

ANDREW. The storm's coming. *(The phone rings. They don't move to answer.)* It's the Lancasters. Lafcad has to speak to them. Let him explain. I can't; it makes no sense. It's inexcusably rude, thoughtless and cruel. What could I say? There's nothing to say. *(Willow enters and answers the phone.)*

WILLOW. Hello. Just one minute. Andrew, it's Mr. Lancaster.

ANDREW. Fine. I'll take it. Here, let me. I'll take it. *(Willow hands him the phone.)* Hello, Mr. Lancaster, this is Andrew. Yes, sir. No, sir. I'm sorry, sir. *(Andrew moves upstage to talk. Willow and Kap start to dance. Flash of lightning; thunder. Willow looks at Kap. The rain starts to fall. A downpour. Lights fade to black.)*

Scene 2

The following fall. Early morning. Baites' backwoods farmhouse. Blue teal season. A wooden picnic table with a bench on the upstage side and worn chairs scattered about the yard. Uncle Baites sits in a chair reading Homer's Iliad *in Greek. Andrew enters from the back porch of the house.*

ANDREW. Where's Willow?

UNCLE BAITES. She didn't want to eat with Maude.

ANDREW. Ah, well … Everyone's eating at different times. I ate early in the dark. I heard them get up for the hunt. They left and I had breakfast by myself in the dark. I have a new theory. Everyone should sleep less. I go to bed fifteen minutes later and set my clock fifteen minutes earlier. You cannot imagine what can be done with three and a half extra hours in the week. That's fourteen hours a month. A whole day's worth of work on "things you don't have time for." Without this plan I would not have won the primary. It's the small things in life. *(Willow enters from the woods. She wears comfortable boots and carries an empty cup of coffee.)* There she is!

WILLOW. I need more coffee.

ANDREW. I'll bring your breakfast out here. *(Andrew exits into the house.)*

WILLOW. I don't want breakfast but there's nothing I can do. I'll just pretend to eat it. Please, I really need more coffee.

UNCLE BAITES. Certainly. I'll get it. *(Uncle Baites takes her coffee cup and exits into the house.)*

WILLOW. Bless you, Uncle Baites. Oh, oh, oh. *(Willow sits down on the picnic table and shakes her hair. Lafcad enters from the house. Lafcad wears old clothes he has found and cobbled together.)*

LAFCAD. Excuse me, I had to leave the house …

WILLOW. Why?

LAFCAD. They're eating —

WILLOW. What?

LAFCAD. Scrambled eggs.

WILLOW. Is Maude eating them?

LAFCAD. I don't know, I couldn't look.

WILLOW. She claims she doesn't eat anything since the treatments. It's not true. I've seen her eat. Even though they say they "didn't get it all," she's recovering. She's making a comeback.

LAFCAD. She doesn't look well to me. Under that scarf are little sticks of hair.

WILLOW. Daddy's divorcing her. He promised me. He did. I feel so unhappy.

LAFCAD. I feel the same. Andrew continues to berate me about the Lancasters' wedding expenses. He sold all of Mama's perfume bottles to pay for Mary Anna's bridal ensemble. I'm forced to be grateful. Tonight I promised Andrew I'd go to his fundraiser and wave a flag.

WILLOW. He wants us all to go. We have to drive to Canton and eat fried chicken with anyone in the parish who wants some. I think I'm going to leave Andrew. Don't tell anyone. I've written a letter. Do you want to read it?

LAFCAD. No. Don't tell me this. He's my brother.

WILLOW. There's a secret. I'm in love with someone else. I have been; I can't stop.

LAFCAD. Don't tell me. Really, it's still morning. Please. It's not me, is it? You're not in love with me?

WILLOW. What? Oh no.

ANDREW. Willow, breakfast! We've got you some eggs. *(Andrew and Baites enter with plates of food.)*

LAFCAD. They're bringing them here!

ANDREW. And biscuits with honey and bacon.

LAFCAD. Scrambled eggs! Ah! *(Lafcad exits to the woods.)*

UNCLE BAITES. I've got fresh coffee.

WILLOW. Thanks. Has she eaten anything?

ANDREW. What?

WILLOW. That woman?

ANDREW. I think she has.

WILLOW. I knew it. *(Loud exploding sound.)*

ANDREW. What's that?!

UNCLE BAITES. Georgia. She's shooting off her potato cannon.

ANDREW. My God. Isn't it against the law?

UNCLE BAITES. I don't know.

ANDREW. I have to be very careful about legalities at this point. The office of State Auditor is all about honesty and trust. I've got no wiggle room. Even though I'm ahead in the polls I'm not cocky. If I win my first election I'll be full of gratitude. The speech that I wrote for tonight is … What do you think, Willow? You've heard my speech.

WILLOW. It's good.

ANDREW. "Powerful." You said it was "powerful."

WILLOW. Yes. Did I? I'm taking in my plate. I'm finished.

ANDREW. Let me.

WILLOW. No. *(Willow exits to the house. The potato cannon is fired again.)*

ANDREW. You should stop her.

UNCLE BAITES. She does it all the time. Scares off predators, snakes and whatnot. I'm thinking I had this thought that I'd ask her to marry me.

ANDREW. What?

UNCLE BAITES. Alright, I won't. I … just so you won't think I'm completely … there's an obscure logic. If we're married, Social Services can't pick her up and force her to go home. It's very ugly, her home situation. Heartbreaking stuff. I bought her a ring.

ANDREW. What ring?

UNCLE BAITES. A diamond. I think I paid too much because I can't bargain. I can't bear to talk to a salesperson. They only want to sell you things and it's so upsetting. This buzzing comes into my ears and I pay whatever they want. Whatever they require I let them have it.

ANDREW. How much did you spend on the ring?

UNCLE BAITES. The price. What it cost.

ANDREW. You paid retail? Full price.

UNCLE BAITES. Yes.

ANDREW. We can return it. Bring it to me and I'll return it. Did you keep the receipt?

UNCLE BAITES. Just the ring in the blue velvet box.

ANDREW. Please get it.

UNCLE BAITES. Yes. I suppose I must. Mustn't I? *(He doesn't go but stands, undecided.)*

ANDREW. Uncle Baites, this girl could be anyone. You let this strange child-person move into your house and now you've gotten her a diamond ring! People may think that you and this girl … things could be construed … It would destroy Daddy's chance for early parole.

BAITES. It's thought he'll get early parole?

ANDREW. His lawyers say he could be out by spring. If all "strings are pulled." He'll be free and whatever indiscretion he may or may not have committed will be viewed as a minor peccadillo. If only we hadn't become impoverished in the process. Daddy will regain status in the community. He's irresistible when he wants to be. Our lives only seem to be devastated but really they're not. People in the end will forget.

BAITES. Of course, you're right, of course. I can't afford diamonds.

ANDREW. Bless you, Uncle Baites. Bless you. *(Baites exits to the house. Andrew takes out a notebook and pen and begins to write. Sound of potato cannon exploding. Andrew notes it and continues writing feverishly. Maude enters from the house. She wears a scarf around her bald head and walks with a cane. It is obvious she has been ill.)*

MAUDE. Hello.

ANDREW. Hello.

MAUDE. I came out for a smoke.

ANDREW. You still smoke?

MAUDE. I do.

ANDREW. Doesn't it make you sick? *(Maude lights up the cigarette.)*

MAUDE. How long does it take to hunt a duck?

ANDREW. I don't know. It depends. Kap usually bags a limit fast.

But he'll stay and watch. Watch the birds in flight.

MAUDE. It feels funny.

ANDREW. What?

MAUDE. To know you're going to die. I mean we all know it but I know it clearly. There's something … it's exhilarating. I love my husband. Most people don't think I do but I wanted to say it so someone would hear it. And I did marry him for money. I did that too. How's the election coming?

ANDREW. Good. You'll be at the fundraiser tonight?

MAUDE. Yes, I'm looking forward to hearing your speech.

ANDREW. It's a marvelous occasion. Tonight for my final fundraiser and rally my family unites! The Clays; the Chrystals. It's clear we'll overcome the travails of the past and come to a brighter future. I just wish my daddy could be with us and hear my speech … but he can't. It's like that, I'm afraid.

MAUDE. Sorry.

ANDREW. This will help him if I'm elected. They'll most certainly give him early parole. People will recognize that he's a good man. That he raised responsible, honest sons.

MAUDE. You look like him when you frown.

ANDREW. What?

MAUDE. The forehead. The wrinkle right here.

ANDREW. You know him?

MAUDE. Some friends knew him. I tuned his piano. The Steinway.

ANDREW. We sold that, the Steinway. It's all gone. The family home, Mama's Italian birdbath. Her collection of glass. Nothing's left. I thought you were a nurse.

MAUDE. Yes.

ANDREW. You tuned Daddy's piano?

MAUDE. On the side I tuned pianos. It was an occasional thing I did. He has perfect pitch.

ANDREW. What?

MAUDE. Your father.

ANDREW. Yes. Kap has it too. He says … Kap says I can't carry a tune. I try to sing softly but I want to sing loud.

MAUDE. What do you sing?

ANDREW. The old tunes.

MAUDE. Such as?

ANDREW. I don't know, really. I like … "Nice Work If You Can

Get It." *(Lafcad enters from the woods carrying a bucket of crawfish.)*
LAFCAD. Barbaric. It's barbaric. *(Georgia enters. She has a new prosthetic leg and can move very fast. She carries a potato cannon.)*
GEORGIA. Give me those! Lafcad!
LAFCAD. No, I can't bear it. Finally, I cannot. She's shooting crawfish out of her cannon. *(Lafcad picks up a writhing crawfish dripping with water.)* They're alive!
GEORGIA. I'm out of potatoes.
LAFCAD. That was a ten-pound bag!
GEORGIA. Give me those!
LAFCAD. No!
GEORGIA. I don't understand! Last night you ate bowl after bowl; sucked them right out of their shells, after they'd been slowly boiled to death. It's better being blasted out of a cannon. Real quick and you don't get sucked!
LAFCAD. *(To Andrew.)* Tell her something. She's not civilized.
ANDREW. It's against the law. Shooting that thing is against the law and you should be stopped. It's very dangerous!
GEORGIA. The state of Louisiana does not consider the potato cannon a firearm. You do not need a license to own one. I know the rules on this shit.
LAFCAD. I'll get you jellybeans. It's extravagant but I'll get you jellybeans to shoot.
GEORGIA. Alright, let's get them. You shoot 'em and all these colors fly out in the sky and get caught up in trees!
MAUDE. Let's see it. *(Maude strolls away from the group and starts putting lipstick on her lips without looking in a mirror.)*
LAFCAD. *(To Andrew.)* Could I borrow some money?
ANDREW. How much?
LAFCAD. Twenty dollars.
ANDREW. Twenty dollars worth of jellybeans?
LAFCAD. Ten won't be enough.
ANDREW. Are you thinking of getting a job?
LAFCAD. Please, please.
ANDREW. Does the question offend you? I think I have a right to ask. Because here I stand, singed and burnt from putting out all your fires and you have done nothing but hide here doing nothing … jobless, penniless, dressing oddly and I want to know what you're doing. I don't know what you're doing and I think I should know.
LAFCAD. I'm gathering myself. Embracing the chaos and what-

not. I can't deal with employment.

GEORGIA. Your brother's lazy. He won't work in the garden. Hasn't pulled up a carrot or washed a potato.

ANDREW. We don't understand each other. Lafcad majored in archaic philosophies. They were all so confused. Like, "negative abilities"? What can you do with negative abilities?

LAFCAD. It's capabilities.

ANDREW. *(To Lafcad.)* You never could explain.

LAFCAD. It's simply that to insist on knowing things through mere fact and reason and sense — eschewing mystery, doubt and uncertainty — bodes emotional, mental and spiritual decrepitude.

ANDREW. I don't know what you are saying.

LAFCAD. Because you do not have the mental capaciousness to grasp any form of paradox. To every question you proclaim an answer.

ANDREW. I can't give you money for jellybeans.

LAFCAD. Fine. I'm voting for Howard Duff.

ANDREW. That's blackmail. And I won't buy your vote. Not yours or anyone's. *(Ed enters with blue teal ducks strung on leather hanging around his shoulders. All gasp, amazed.)*

ED. 'Morning. Back from the hunt. Pretty birds right here. Pretty birds.

ANDREW. Look at those.

ED. Blue teal are small birds. Not easy to hit with the steel shot. Missed 'em once or twice.

ANDREW. Amazing.

ED. My first time out I bagged the limit. *(Kap enters, looking menacing.)* Next month mallard season starts. I want me some of those big puddle ducks. Kap's my man. Good dog he's got out there in the truck. Ace. Crackerjack retriever. Swam out in some cold ugly swamp water. Carried back bird after bird. Soft as you please.

ANDREW. You use the duck call Willow gave you?

ED. Give the hen the comeback call and 'round she came, bringing down the whole flock. They're lucky we didn't shoot all of 'em that came back our way. Where's Willow? I want her to see this. Make her proud.

ANDREW. I think she's inside.

ED. I'll get her to help me clean and gut these for supper. We eat duck tonight.

ANDREW. Let's eat early. I mean my rally's at eight. It'll take us seventeen minutes to drive to Canton. It's imperative I arrive at least twenty minutes beforehand to be courteous, to show enthusiasm.

ED. We won't forget you, boy. You're our candidate. Right now these ducks need tending.

MAUDE. I'll help clean them. I know how.

ED. I wanna show these to Willow. You know how she is about you. Christ, I've told you to leave off! *(Ed exits to the house.)*

MAUDE. I think I'm ... walking. I'm walking, I'm walking, I'm walking, I'm walking, I'm walking. *(Maude exits to the woods.)*

GEORGIA. He didn't shoot those ducks.

ANDREW. What do you mean?

KAP. He's a fuck! Unbelievable. Shot two of my decoys to smithereens. Almost hit my dog. I had to confiscate his duck call. Sounded like some prehistoric dying shit. I'll never be able to hunt that hole again. He shot one duck. One. A cripple. Ace brings it in to him and Ed just watches it writhe in pain, won't break its neck, doesn't know how, finally he stands back and shoots it again. Fucking shoots it again. Not much of that bird left to cook for supper. And he's back here claiming he bagged the limit. I'd be ashamed saying I killed what I didn't kill. Why is he alive?! What does he hope to accomplish by being alive?! People like that have no right to breathe.

ANDREW. Yeah. Okay. But I mean he's the sport; you're the guide. He's paying your top daily rate. Just be polite.

KAP. And you just be impolite. Forget he's backing your campaign and paying my rate and tell me what you really think of that lying fuck. Tell me something real, Andrew, 'cause I'm sick of bullshit! You're up to your eyes in it! You know that?! You know?!

ANDREW. I can't — when you're like this ... I can't ...

KAP. Like what?! Like fucking what?! Fucking what am I like?!

ANDREW. Just shut up.

KAP. You shut up! You shut up! You shut up!

ANDREW. Fine! *(Andrew starts to go.)*

LAFCAD. How about the twenty dollars?

ANDREW. I can't! Get a job! You need to get a job for your own sake! I'm tired of this family's behavior. It's abhorrent to my nature! Every fiber of my being! *(Andrew exits to the house. All fume.)*

GEORGIA. I want those jellybeans. *(Kap picks up the notebook Andrew left.)*

KAP. *(As he reads the notebook.)* Okay. Well, shit. This is ... Oh man. This stuff and it's all in his tight little, perfect little, pinched-up writing.

LAFCAD. What?

KAP. *(Reading from the notebook.)* "My daily affirmation. I, Andrew Clay, am a powerful man. I visualize a mansion and me with a crown on my head and a medal around my neck. I am the most powerful man in Louisiana. I am respected on a global level."

LAFCAD. He has to be stopped. He's envisioning himself as a sovereign.

KAP. It's embarrassing.

GEORGIA. He needs to eat a bug.

LAFCAD. What?

GEORGIA. Whenever someone in my family got too know-it-all-uppity, we'd sit on 'em and make 'em eat a bug.

KAP. What kind?

GEORGIA. Usually a cockroach.

KAP. Let's do it.

LAFCAD. He won't eat a bug. We can't make him eat a bug. He's too strong.

GEORGIA. I'll fix it on a cracker. Chop it up, add some stuff and tell him it's a snack. I'll bet he'll eat it 'cause he's so polite.

KAP. Do it.

LAFCAD. This is humorous.

GEORGIA. Come on, let's go.

LAFCAD. We'll see if Andrew will eat a bug just to be polite. It's so funny. Oh my God. *(Georgia, Lafcad, and Kap are leaving as Willow enters from around the house.)*

WILLOW. Kap!

KAP. What? *(Georgia and Lafcad exit.)*

WILLOW. Wait.

KAP. What?

WILLOW. I saw y'all got back. I have to talk to you. I have a letter. I wrote a letter to Andrew.

KAP. What letter?

WILLOW. I told him … Because the truth is my heart … Tell me it will be alright.

KAP. Okay, sure. What's wrong?

WILLOW. Don't you know? … I can't talk. There's so much to say. Don't you think there is? *(A silence.)* Do you think I'm pretty?

KAP. Very pretty. Yes.

29

WILLOW. When you look at me I feel that way. Do you ever think about me?

KAP. Yeah. I have. I do. Willow.

WILLOW. I'm putting the letter in Andrew's notebook. I'm putting it here for him to find. *(Willow puts a letter into Andrew's notebook.)* My life is a fraud. I live at war with my thoughts and feelings, all of them. Tell me you know that.

KAP. You're not a fraud. I don't see it. I just think ... everything's fine, sort of.

WILLOW. You mean fine how it is or fine how it could be? *(A beat.)* Please tell me.

KAP. I can't say. You know that. All along. You know.

ED. *(Offstage.)* Willow! Willow! *(Ed enters from the house.)* There you are! I wanted to show you the harvest. Blue teal. Laid out in the kitchen all across the counter. I used the duck call you gave me. It brought 'em all in, right, Kap?

KAP. No, sorry, Ed. I'm not standing here and doing that shit. *(Kap exits.)*

WILLOW. *(To Kap.)* What's wrong? *(To Ed.)* What's wrong with him?

ED. Arrogant, I guess. Doesn't understand he's in the service industry. You and Andy need money?

WILLOW. Of course but Andy won't borrow anymore.

ED. I'll put something in your account. A nice gift. Look, I know what I said about divorce but Maude's been sick. I can't get rid of her now she's sick. It's common decency.

WILLOW. She's not that sick.

ED. Baby, she's gonna die.

WILLOW. When?

ED. How'd you get so hard? Maude did nothing to your mother but care for her, clean her, feed her, fix her hair, do her nails.

WILLOW. The first time I saw her sitting in the kitchen wearing a blue smock with her hair pulled back in a ponytail and a stetho-scope around her neck, I thought, she's not a nurse. She was put-ting sugar in her coffee, wearing lipstick and smoking a cigarette and I thought, she's not a nurse.

ED. Hey! I would only have a top-of-the-line paid professional RN take care of your mother. You understand me?! Is that clear?!

WILLOW. How could you let her touch my mama after she touched you?! I don't know how you could! She wasn't even a nurse. *(Andrew enters from the house.)*

ANDREW. Where's my notebook? I have some new ideas for the speech. I want to include a boyhood memory. Ah, here it is! *(To the notebook.)* I must never lose you again! Never, never!

WILLOW. Andy, there's a letter inside your notebook. Wait to read it.

ANDREW. Wait for what?

WILLOW. Until you're alone. Not with him. *(Willow exits.)*

ED. Ungrateful; spoiled. She's concocted some story. Thinks Maude and me had some involvement … but none of that was until after Emma died. Maybe it seemed sudden, the wedding, but we came together in our grief. The grief brought us together.

ANDREW. I think for Willow it was, you know, too soon. *(Ed experiences a flash of fury.)*

ED. Your uncle's got good timberland out here that's running to seed. I could get in some workers. Thin and cut, remove large pines, select hardwood. Get some herbicide to stunt grass and weeds. Give him a nice income. I don't understand your wife. Her head's not right. She claims Maude wasn't a nurse! Sat right here and said that to me. I'm counting on you to tell her the truth.

ANDREW. What truth?

ED. You know it. I just told you. *(A beat.)* I enjoy backing your campaign. I'm glad to do it. Having all my friends and colleagues help you out is something I wanna do.

ANDREW. And I'm grateful for all your help. I really am.

ED. I consider you a loyal friend, just like your daddy. I can count on your daddy in every way. We understand each other and if nothing runs amuck he'll be out this spring. We don't want bumps. You make her come 'round. You tell her Maude's a registered nurse; the best in her field.

ANDREW. Ed, I'm feeling … Maybe I'm just imagining something that's not there.

ED. No, it's there.

ANDREW. I hope you understand. It's not something, all your help, I can pay back. In any way. I'm an honest man. I think I'd make a good State Auditor. I'm a hard worker with a clear vision. I can make state finances work. I want to serve people.

ED. *(A beat.)* However you wanna say it. It's okay. I know who raised you. I know your roots. Now how you like your duck prepared? Barbecue? Smoked? A lá Orange? Which one?

31

ANDREW. You choose.

ED. I'll surprise you. *(Ed exits. Andrew picks up his notebook. The letter slips out. He opens Willow's letter and reads it. His face floods with emotion. He gasps for breath. Lafcad and Kap enter from the house. Andrew conceals the letter.)*

LAFCAD. No, Kap, Kap, it's really delicious. I've tried it before.

KAP. It looks disgusting.

LAFCAD. It's considered a delicacy up around Bogue Chitto. Andrew, you'll have some?

ANDREW. What?

LAFCAD. Georgia's prepared this snack; it's a home recipe. *(Georgia enters with a tray.)*

GEORGIA. Hi! I got it. Anyone want some Crispy Spicy Cracker Snack?

LAFCAD. Love them. Please.

KAP. Sure. *(They palm the crackers and feign eating them. Improvising how good they taste.)*

GEORGIA. *(Offering one to Andrew.)* Andrew?

ANDREW. Yes. *(Lost in thought, Andrew takes a cracker, eats it, chews and swallows. The others suppress hysterical laughter.)*

LAFCAD. More?

GEORGIA. Sure.

KAP. Oh yeah. *(She passes out crackers and stops at Andrew.)*

GEORGIA. Andrew?

ANDREW. Thanks. *(Andrew takes a cracker. He takes a bite and coughs softly.)* Excuse me … I … I … *(Andrew spits out a glob of cracker and bug.)* So sorry. It's not the … *(He indicates the crackers.)* Excellent cracker. *(Andrew coughs, chokes, and spits up bug. It is as though he were coughing up his heart. Baites enters and sees Andrew's great distress.)*

BAITES. Andrew! *(Baites tries to pat Andrew on the back.)*

ANDREW. I'm so … forgive me … I'm fine. It's fine. I'm perfectly … *(Andrew exits coughing and spitting. All except Baites collapse with laughter.)*

LAFCAD. Oh my God, that's so funny.

KAP. I can't believe, two!

LAFCAD. He ate two!

UNCLE BAITES. Two what?

KAP. You don't want to know.

LAFCAD. It's … he ate … My God, it was her idea.

UNCLE BAITES. What?

GEORGIA. Don't tell him!

UNCLE BAITES. Tell me!

GEORGIA. No, please!

UNCLE BAITES. What was it? I want to know!

KAP. Just a dumb, a stupid joke.

LAFCAD. Hilarious.

GEORGIA. It was mean; it was so mean!

UNCLE BAITES. What? Tell me! It didn't look funny.

GEORGIA. See, he'll hate me if he hears, he'll stop liking me, don't tell him!

LAFCAD. For goodness' sake, it's not that bad, we just fed Andrew a bug.

UNCLE BAITES. A bug? Why?

LAFCAD. To be deranged.

UNCLE BAITES. Good Lord. *(Baites looks disturbed.)*

GEORGIA. See, he doesn't like me now. I told you he wouldn't! I'm nothing he should like!

UNCLE BAITES. Such foolishness! I like you, I like you! Here, I got you a ring!

GEORGIA. What?

UNCLE BAITES. Look. *(Baites produces the ring. He gives it to her. She opens the box and shows it around. Maude enters from the woods. She doesn't join the group but stands by a tree putting on lipstick.)*

LAFCAD. My God. Is that a real diamond? Is it real?

UNCLE BAITES. Yes.

LAFCAD. But why? I don't understand. You're not proposing, I hope?

UNCLE BAITES. Of course not. I wouldn't do that, something like that.

GEORGIA. Should I give it back?

UNCLE BAITES. Do whatever you want with it. Throw it in the swamp. I just wanted you to have it because I'm ridiculous. *(Baites exits to the woods.)*

LAFCAD. I think he's, well, he's …

KAP. Upset.

GEORGIA. Should I give back the ring?

LAFCAD. Yes.

GEORGIA. But I want it.

LAFCAD. Take it off your finger and give it back. It's too extravagant. He's already given you a leg.

GEORGIA. Yeah. Okay. I'll give it back. *(Georgia exits to the woods.)*

KAP. I'm leaving.

LAFCAD. *(To Kap.)* Aren't you staying for Andrew's rally?

KAP. No.

LAFCAD. You told Andrew you'd stay.

KAP. Just here for the ducks.

LAFCAD. Andrew wants us all here. A united front.

KAP. I'm not staying. *(Maude moves in to them.)*

MAUDE. *(To Kap.)* Could you drop me off at Covington?

KAP. Sure.

LAFCAD. You're not staying either?

MAUDE. No. I'm going home.

LAFCAD. What about Ed?

MAUDE. He won't give a shit.

KAP. Let's go. I'm ready. I've had enough. *(Maude and Kap exit.)*

LAFCAD. *(Calling after them.)* Tell someone you're leaving. I don't want them asking me. I'll pretend I don't know. I have seen not a thing. *(Lafcad reflects a moment and smiles to himself.)* Lafcadio. Lafcad. Lafcadio. *(Willow enters from the woods.)* Willow, do you know how I got the name Lafcad? Originally my mother, with her classic flair, gave me the name Laurence Keats Clay. But everyone, I don't know why, started calling me "Larry." Do I look like a "Larry"? So I changed it to Lafcad in honor, of course, of Lafcadio Hearn, the somewhat macabre nineteenth century journalist.

WILLOW. Have you seen Kap?

LAFCAD. He's gone. He took her, Maude, with him. *(Willow rushes upstage and sees Kap and Maude leaving together.)*

WILLOW. They're leaving together.

LAFCAD. Don't tell anyone, I'm pretending I don't know. I know nothing.

WILLOW. About what?

LAFCAD. Transgressions.

WILLOW. Kap and —

LAFCAD. Shh. *(Andrew enters.)*

ANDREW. Excuse me, I —

LAFCAD. How's the cough?

ANDREW. Fine.

LAFCAD. Good, good. Kap and Maude have gone. They won't

be here for your rally.

ANDREW. They won't?

LAFCAD. No.

ANDREW. Why?

LAFCAD. I'm pretending I don't know. *(Lafcad exits whistling.)*

ANDREW. I read it. I read the letter.

WILLOW. Please forget everything I wrote.

ANDREW. You love someone else.

WILLOW. None of it's true. Believe me.

ANDREW. I really ... I didn't know things were wrong.

WILLOW. Of course. Nothing's wrong. It's not wrong.

ANDREW. Because I always thought, we're the lucky ones. We're the lucky ones.

WILLOW. I thought so, yes. I thought we are.

ANDREW. Tell me we are.

WILLOW. We're the lucky ones. *(Georgia enters from the woods. She is admiring the diamond ring that is on her finger.)*

GEORGIA. It's mine! It's all mine! Baites said for me to keep it and wear it on this finger. It means we're engaged.

WILLOW. Oh my. It's not real, is it? *(Willow looks at the ring on Georgia's hand.)*

ANDREW. Yes it is. It really is. It's real. *(Lights fade to black.)*

End of Act One

ACT TWO

Scene 1

Kap's cabin, deep in the woods. The following winter. Late afternoon. Kap moves around the cabin eloquently practicing duck calls. He has been drinking scotch.

Maude is at a butcher block, cleaning and gutting mallards. Her health has greatly improved. She has never looked more alive.

KAP. The three most important things you have to take on a duck hunt — I don't care whether it is saltwater, freshwater, swamp. You have to have a gun, you have to have some shells, some bullets to kill the duck. And after that the next thing I'd take would be this. *(He indicates duck call.)* Over waders, over decoys, over dogs, over anything. Because if you know how to use it right, many times you can bring that duck right to you with nothing else around. They're hearing the sound and they're looking for the ducks and even if they don't see them, they come to the sound. And you can bring 'em in range to kill them. After guns and shells that would be the next thing. Takes years to learn to do it right. You can learn how to sound like a duck pretty quickly, but then the next part is you're actually talking to those birds. When they're coming in you pick a bird, you watch how that bird responds. Even if there're a hundred birds, I'm talking to that one bird. In those flocks there'll be some dominant bird that'll kind of control the flock. A lot of time it's a big ol' hen. She decides whether they're going to light or not light. I'm talking to that one bird. Convincing her to come to me. Basically it goes: demand, beg, plead. *(Kap blows on his duck call: demand, beg, plead.)* It's entirely an illusion.
MAUDE. Have you decided?
KAP. Yes.
MAUDE. You won't hurt him?

36

KAP. No.

MAUDE. He wants to use knives. He wants first blood and that's all. A scratch. That's all. *(A pause. Kap pours himself a large scotch.)*

KAP. You don't have to clean those birds.

MAUDE. I want to; it calms me. If you don't mind.

KAP. Go ahead.

MAUDE. I don't like asking. It's strange, I know. This deceit. *(A beat.)* The reason I love my husband is he lies. I understand people who do that. They have so many people they want to please. These liars. *(Kap blows on the duck call.)* The daughter wore me down. How he dotes on her and fears her. *(Kap finishes the scotch.)* I didn't know what I was doing. I never meant for Ed to find out anything.

KAP. Then how did he? *(Kap puts on his coat.)*

MAUDE. Where are you going?

KAP. To work with the dogs.

MAUDE. What if he comes?

KAP. I'm out with the dogs. You should go. If he finds you here and cuts your throat ... I don't want the memories.

MAUDE. I'll clean up and go.

KAP. And don't tell Andrew. Don't tell him you asked me to do this.

MAUDE. Why would I? Kap, please. Are you mad at me?

KAP. Shit, Maude, come on. *(Kap exits. Maude starts to clean up the mallards. Her cell phone rings. She wipes off her hands and answers it.)*

MAUDE. *(Into phone.)* Hello ... I'm in my car. I'm shopping ... Yes, I am. For dinner. Where are you? ... Ed, please don't go out there. It's over. It meant nothing. It was the illness, all the medicines ... Yes, I know your family code and ... Yes, yes, your genetic compunction ... Do it then. A touch, a scratch. Only that. And tell no one. Please. No one's to know ... Lamb chops ... Yes, I know you do, that's why I'm getting them ... Rare, yes ... 'Bye. *(Maude clicks off the phone. She prepares to leave. There is knocking at the door. Maude gasps. She quickly climbs a wooden ladder and hides in the loft under some canvas.)*

UNCLE BAITES. *(Offstage, knocking.)* Kap?! Are you home? Kap? *(Uncle Baites and Lafcad enter.)*

LAFCAD. Kap? Kap, are you here?

UNCLE BAITES. *(Noting the dead mallards.)* He's around. Look at this. Mallards. Ugh.

UNCLE BAITES. It's cold in here. Freezing.

LAFCAD. Kap loves the cold. I'll put something in the stove.

UNCLE BAITES. His gun's here.

LAFCAD. *(Putting wood in the stove.)* This will help. I think we can burn this. It seems burnable.

UNCLE BAITES. I'm sorry to get you out of work.

LAFCAD. I'm a waiter. What do I care? I'm serving food.

UNCLE BAITES. Ed's call got me worried. He sounded … It was this primal tone. I started giving him directions to Kap's cabin, and then I stopped because something terrible came over me. I think he did the wife.

LAFCAD. What?

UNCLE BAITES. Kap. The wife. Ed's wife.

LAFCAD. Of course, yes. Kap's unstable that way. I mean he's never been engaged. We've been engaged. Me once. You twice.

UNCLE BAITES. Yes.

LAFCAD. It didn't work out. But we made a step.

UNCLE BAITES. I'm wondering where he is. Ed's a vengeful man. Comes from deep backwoods trash. They cut people, leave a mark.

LAFCAD. For what?

UNCLE BAITES. Transgressions. *(Baites opens the back door and goes out into the yard.)* Kap! You around, sugar? You here? Kap! Where is he? *(There is no answer. Baites returns to the cabin. He goes to warm himself by the fire.)* Kap needs to get a phone.

LAFCAD. He doesn't like to talk. What is there to say? We're all so separate.

UNCLE BAITES. You've become very glum.

LAFCAD. It's the employment. I go table to table — the pick-up window — the dessert tray. Receipts. *(A beat.)* There's such loneliness.

UNCLE BAITES. Yes. I miss Georgia.

LAFCAD. She was fun.

UNCLE BAITES. I'll never forgive Andrew for exposing her. Scaring her away. Contemptible.

LAFCAD. I agree.

UNCLE BAITES. I need to stop clenching my jaw. What can we drink?

LAFCAD. *(Taking out bottles.)* He's got Jack Daniels, Wild Turkey and scotch. No Cokes. I don't see any Cokes.

UNCLE BAITES. Jack Daniels double. Here, I'll pour my own.

LAFCAD. Here's soda water, crackers. Some suspect cheese.

UNCLE BAITES. It's just so sickening, all the regret. How's your father?

LAFCAD. They're releasing him. He has a release date. This April he'll be free.

UNCLE BAITES. My God, he's an operator, your daddy. A chronic charmer.

LAFCAD. When he gets out he'll have no place to go. He refuses to stay with me or Andrew. He says I'm a "flake" and Andrew's a "toadying hypocrite." He wants to live here in the woods with Kap. Kap doesn't want him.

UNCLE BAITES. Why not?

LAFCAD. Kap says he lied to Mama.

UNCLE BAITES. About what?

LAFCAD. Money, women, and property.

UNCLE BAITES. Yes, I pretended I didn't know. It would have embarrassed Madeline terribly. I pretended I didn't know.

LAFCAD. At night there were horrible, screaming fights.

UNCLE BAITES. Oh God.

LAFCAD. In the morning Mama told me, "We only fight because your daddy won't dance with me anymore." At the time I believed her. But of course there was more.

UNCLE BAITES. Madeline was a sublime dancer. Her one great pleasure, moving through space.

LAFCAD. She danced with me. We took lessons together.

UNCLE BAITES. Today's the eighth anniversary of her death.

LAFCAD. Really? I forgot. I forgot.

UNCLE BAITES. Yes, why remember the sorrow.

LAFCAD. I'm sure Andrew sent flowers. Kap always remembers. He drinks scotch all day and does something insane. We all knew Mama loved him best.

UNCLE BAITES. She said he'd capture the world.

LAFCAD. He moved out here when she died. Gave up his research on indigenous water weeds and never came back. (*Hold a moment. A knock on the door.*)

ANDREW. (*Offstage.*) Kap? You home? It's me.

LAFCAD. Andrew. (*Lafcad opens the door.*) Hi. Kap's not here. We're here. (*Baites and Andrew look at each other. There is a great tension between them.)*

ANDREW. Uncle Baites.

UNCLE BAITES. I'm leaving.

ANDREW. This can't go on.

UNCLE BAITES. I'll get a go-cup for the road. Something plastic and big. *(Baites haplessly looks for a plastic cup to take his drink on the road.)*

ANDREW. I was trying to help you. I thought you were going to thank me. I deserve some thanks. I got back your ring.

UNCLE BAITES. I didn't want it back. I'd given it to her. It was a present.

ANDREW. It infuriates me how you don't want to be helped when I'm helping you! I get no gratitude, no consideration. *(Baites comes and pushes Andrew in the chest.)*

UNCLE BAITES. You self-satisfied man!

ANDREW. I don't understand! Would you want me to deceive you and keep it all a secret?

UNCLE BAITES. Yes, yes! Now I'm alone.

ANDREW. She was a liar. Almost twenty-five years old and the mother of six!

UNCLE BAITES. Children she had forced on her from age twelve! One leg taken! Would you have her give up two?

ANDREW. I wasn't wrong to warn you! And I'm sick of your ingratitude!

UNCLE BAITES. I'm going to hurt him.

LAFCAD. Go. Go. Take the bottle and go! *(Lafcad hands Baites the Jack Daniels bottle.)*

UNCLE BAITES. *(To Lafcad.)* Warn your brother.

ANDREW. Warn me what?

UNCLE BAITES. Not you. I wouldn't warn you.

ANDREW. I don't understand. Did you want to be made out a raging old fool?! *(Baites comes at Andrew waving the bottle.)*

UNCLE BAITES. I'll shatter you! I'll shatter!

LAFCAD. Stop! Don't! Go, Uncle Baites. You know I can't bear anything. This is too much for me; I have conditions.

UNCLE BAITES. I'm going. I'll hurt him. I'll leave. *(Baites exits out the front door.)*

LAFCAD. I'm locking the door. In case he returns.

ANDREW. I could break his jaw so easily but I wouldn't. I wouldn't.

LAFCAD. Why do you...?

ANDREW. What?! Why do I what? Don't you think I should have told him his fiancée was an imposter? I don't understand how else you could think. There's no other way to think.

LAFCAD. I think ... Don't tell him I spoke but I think he ... There were feelings he had for her.

ANDREW. Absurd feelings, yes. People shouldn't have feelings like that.

LAFCAD. Do you know where Georgia is now?

ANDREW. She never returned to Tunica to help raise her six children. The three different fathers are doing that. Or their mothers. Someone. Not Georgia, or whatever her real name is. Why do people pretend?

LAFCAD. She wanted a change. Something better.

ANDREW. She left six children. She left six children for "a change"!

LAFCAD. Yes, because ... Who can say? People don't know anything. They can't discern motive. The paradoxes of motive.

ANDREW. Really, Lafcad, there are things in this world that are right and wrong. It's not all a fog. Where's Kap?

LAFCAD. I don't know. Why are you here?

ANDREW. I left something. A blue notebook. Very careless. I must find it. *(He starts to hunt around for the notebook.)*

LAFCAD. You've been out here?

ANDREW. Some. Yes.

LAFCAD. You never come here. *(Andrew searches for his notebook, under books and furniture, through drawers and cabinets.)*

ANDREW. I've needed someplace quiet. I'm wrestling with thoughts, new policies. There are a lot of pressures being State Auditor. Realities that could not have been foreseen. You can make all the rules and laws in the world, but if you don't have the resources to enforce accountability you're going nowhere. And there are interest groups. I'm not immune. Ed has strong viewpoints he wants me to consider, and it isn't always easy to maintain clear objectivity. I have high standards. He knows that. But some decisions I make I think he could have influenced just because ... proximity. I mean, his financial backing, his daughter ... There's access, proximity. I struggle.

LAFCAD. *(Putting rotten cheese on a cracker.)* We all do.

ANDREW. How's your new job?

41

LAFCAD. Interesting. People tip me. I'm tipped.

ANDREW. That's good.

LAFCAD. Usually it's a small tip because the service is deliberately bad.

ANDREW. You'll get fired. They'll fire you.

LAFCAD. They're taking their time. They want to believe I'm sincere.

ANDREW. How you act I don't understand.

LAFCAD. I feel the same.

ANDREW. Why are you here?

LAFCAD. To see Kap.

ANDREW. About what?

LAFCAD. Just something.

ANDREW. You don't want to talk about it with me. You'll tell him but you won't tell me. Why am I always on the outside?

LAFCAD. You're not alone on the outside. We're all present.

ANDREW. Kap doesn't have any money to lend you.

LAFCAD. Money? Why would I need money? I've no intention of being solvent. *(There is a thump from the loft.)*

ANDREW. What's that?

LAFCAD. Something's up there.

ANDREW. An animal. It was something.

LAFCAD. Or someone. Do you think it could be someone?

ANDREW. There's no one there. Is there anyone there? *(Andrew tosses a block of wood at the canvas up in the loft. Something moves. A board creaks.)* It's an animal.

LAFCAD. What kind?

ANDREW. Something wild. A squirrel, maybe a rat, a raccoon, maybe a possum. Let's see.

LAFCAD. Will it bite?

ANDREW. Possibly. Let's take protection. *(Lafcad hands Andrew a rifle.)* Not a gun. *(Lafcad grabs an arrow and hands it to Andrew, then picks up an iron fire tool. Andrew starts up the wood ladder that leads to the loft. Lafcad follows with the fire tool. Andrew stops at the top of the ladder, holding the arrow threateningly. He turns and mouths to Lafcad, "It's in here." Lafcad panics and whacks his fire tool down on the canvas repeatedly.)*

MAUDE. Ah! Ah! Stop! Please. Really! *(Maude emerges from the canvas screaming.)*

ANDREW. *(Turning to Lafcad.)* Stop! Lafcad, stop! No more!

(Andrew turns to Lafcad and accidentally stabs him in the shoulder with the arrow. Lafcad falls down the ladder shouting in pain.)

LAFCAD. Ah! I'm pierced! I've been pierced!

ANDREW. Maude, what are you doing? Are you alright?

MAUDE. Help me down from here. I have to go. I have to get out. *(Maude and Andrew come down the ladder. Lafcad walks around in a stupor.)*

LAFCAD. I'm wounded. You thrust an arrow into my flesh. Look. *(Lafcad displays his shoulder and chest.)*

ANDREW. I don't see any blood.

LAFCAD. It's coming, it's coming. The wound is so deep the blood has to travel. *(Maude walks to the back door and goes into the backyard. Andrew follows her.)* Don't leave me here! Jesus Christ, I've been shot with an arrow. *(Lafcad staggers to the bathroom. Outside Andrew stops Maude.)*

ANDREW. Maude, please. Are you hurt? Maude, please.

MAUDE. Go, leave. You have to get out of here.

ANDREW. What's wrong?

MAUDE. We're in danger of losing everything. It has to end. You're married. We're both married. So many people could be hurt.

ANDREW. I know. It's wrong. I love you.

MAUDE. It's over, it's over, it's over. *(She shakes him, then kisses him intensely on the lips.)* Tell me you believe it's over.

ANDREW. Yes.

MAUDE. It's over. Tell me you know.

ANDREW. I know. *(They kiss again.)*

MAUDE. Now go. You have to go. Swear to me, you'll go.

ANDREW. I'll go.

MAUDE. Goodbye. *(Maude exits through the backyard. Andrew goes into the cabin. Lafcad sits with his hand over the wound on his shoulder.)*

ANDREW. Are you alright?

LAFCAD. I don't know.

ANDREW. Let me look. *(Lafcad removes his hand, there is blood.)* Oh my God. There is … It's bleeding. Let me get ice. *(Andrew puts ice into a washcloth.)*

LAFCAD. I feel faint.

ANDREW. *(Putting ice on the wound.)* Here. Here. Oh, Lafcad, I'm so sorry. Forgive me. It was an accident. I didn't mean to hurt you. I just … I'm so sorry. Please, please forgive me.

LAFCAD. Are you crying? Good Lord. It's a flesh wound. A hole.

ANDREW. It never should have happened. I don't know how ...

LAFCAD. That woman Maude ... She was hiding. She didn't want us to find her and suddenly we did. We found her, she was there.

ANDREW. I love her. I'm dying. I'm in love with her. I'm dying.

LAFCAD. What? That woman that was here?

ANDREW. Yes. She came to me one night. Willow and Ed had gone to the Mistletoe MarketPlace in Shreveport and she shows up on my doorstep. This doe-like creature. This incredibly sheltered human being and she's quivering. Her clothes were off in half an hour and she's telling me as clothes are flying how unhappy she is and her life is empty and she must find something. I didn't know what to make of it. But her need. This need she had for something that seemed to be me. And here's the thing I'm going to tell you next. We've been meeting. Here in this cabin. I've told no one. The doctors gave her six months and we thought, what harm can some happiness be? A small slice of happiness. But her health ... I mean her strength increases. Her complexion has become more beautiful than ever, those wonderful rose cheeks.

LAFCAD. I'm confused. Does Kap know about this?

ANDREW. I can't believe I've lied to him. My own brother. Everything's falling apart. I've been lying. I'm not a liar; so it's impossible. But love makes you do the things you do.

LAFCAD. But you and Willow ... Aren't you expecting a child? In May; it's in May.

ANDREW. Yes.

LAFCAD. And it's yours?

ANDREW. Of course it's mine! *(Lafcad slowly reaches up and pulls Andrew's nose.)* What are you doing?

LAFCAD. Pulling your nose. Checking this isn't a rubber mask. That you are my brother, Andrew Jeremiah Clay, and not an imposter.

ANDREW. Fine. *(Lafcad pulls hard on Andrew's nose.)* OW!

LAFCAD. Andrew.

ANDREW. Yes.

LAFCAD. You're in love with Maude Chrystal, Willow's step-mother.

ANDREW. Yes, yes. I don't know how it happened. I've been so alone. She makes me feel like I'm not a fool.

LAFCAD. (*A revelation.*) My God, I can't believe you're telling me this. We're talking like brothers and you're telling me this!

ANDREW. I need to bandage your wounds. Let me find something. Here's a clean rag.

LAFCAD. What does Willow say?

ANDREW. I didn't tell her. I'm hiding it from her.

LAFCAD. Of course, of course. You must.

ANDREW. I've even tried to convince her to accept Maude. I told her she was a nurse.

LAFCAD. Was she a nurse?

ANDREW. No. She told me she wasn't.

LAFCAD. Why was she hired?

ANDREW. She and Ed had been involved for years. I know it's very sordid what people do. Here, I found duct tape. I want to bandage the wound. Stop the bleeding. Let's take off the ice.

LAFCAD. I don't know. I might faint.

ANDREW. Here. Drink some scotch. Straight shot. There you go. (*Lafcad drinks the scotch.*)

LAFCAD. Ugh.

ANDREW. Now quickly. (*Andrew removes the rag with ice and starts to bandage the clean cloth on with duct tape.*)

LAFCAD. Ow.

ANDREW. Hang on.

LAFCAD. That's tight.

ANDREW. It needs to be tight.

LAFCAD. Okay. (*Lafcad takes another swig of scotch.*) Uncle Baites had it wrong.

ANDREW. What?

LAFCAD. He thought Maude and Kap ... We thought they were ...

ANDREW. No, no, it was me. I was the one. Not Kap. Kap isn't always the one.

LAFCAD. Oh God, Ed's coming here! To the cabin!

ANDREW. What for?

LAFCAD. I'm not sure. But he must suspect or know something because Baites said there was something frightening in his voice. He wanted directions to Kap's cabin. We came to warn him.

ANDREW. To warn him. Oh my God. Ed's coming here?!

LAFCAD. That's too tight.

ANDREW. It has to be tight to stop the bleeding.

LAFCAD. My arm's starting to tingle. There's no blood. I feel weak.

ANDREW. Here's ice. *(Andrew hands Lafcad the washcloth with ice. There is blood in the ice.)*

LAFCAD. It's my blood! I feel sick. I'm going to be …

ANDREW. Go! There's the bathroom. Go. *(Lafcad goes into the bathroom. Sound of Lafcad getting sick. Andrew pours himself a drink.)* How did I get in this? How did I get in this? Life's a dream. *(Kap enters the backyard. Andrew drinks scotch. Kap enters the cabin through the back door.)*

KAP. Andrew.

ANDREW. Kap.

KAP. What are you…?

ANDREW. Looking. I was looking. You didn't find a notebook here, did you? A journal I left.

KAP. *(Indicating a drawer.)* I stuck it in there.

ANDREW. *(Finding the journal.)* Ah, here it is. I left it the last time I was here. You were away hunting ducks in Minnesota.

KAP. Canvasbacks.

ANDREW. I needed a respite. All the work.

KAP. Yeah.

ANDREW. Today's the eighth anniversary of Mama's death. I sent flowers to the grave. I signed all of our names. *(A silence.)*

KAP. When you're here don't clean things. Don't make improvements.

ANDREW. I just … there were cobwebs and —

KAP. I like the cobwebs. Look, you should go.

ANDREW. Why?

KAP. I'm busy.

ANDREW. You're busy?

KAP. Andrew, you have to go.

ANDREW. You're upset with me.

KAP. No.

ANDREW. *(Indicating journal.)* Did you read this?

KAP. Some.

ANDREW. So you know.

KAP. Of course I know. I didn't have to read that to know.

ANDREW. I should have been frank with you. About the use of your cabin. You're my brother. And there's something else. I've wounded Lafcad. He's in the bathroom and I've wounded him

46

with an arrow.

KAP. You need to stop telling me this shit.

ANDREW. It was an accident.

KAP. Is that his blood?

ANDREW. Yes.

KAP. *(Going to the bathroom door.)* Lafcad? Lafcad, are you there? *(Kap opens the door. Lafcad has passed out on the bathroom floor.)* He's passed out. Let's get him out. Bring him out. *(They carry Lafcad to the sofa.)* He'll live, right? *(To Lafcad.)* Lafcad, you okay? You okay?

LAFCAD. Not exactly.

KAP. *(About the duct tape.)* What's all this shit?

ANDREW. His bandage.

LAFCAD. I'm woozy. I think it's the scotch.

KAP. Lie here, rest. You'll be okay. *(Lafcad shuts his eyes and leans back. Kap turns to Andrew.)* Why did you do this?

ANDREW. It was an accident. Maude was here and he was hitting her with firewood and I tried to stop him and stabbed him with an arrow. It's hard to explain.

KAP. Maude was here? I told her to leave.

ANDREW. You saw her?

KAP. Yeah. She came here. Cleaned those birds for me. Did a shitty job, said she knew how.

ANDREW. Why was she here?

KAP. *(A beat.)* Ask her.

ANDREW. You're not ...

KAP. What?

ANDREW. Involved. You and Maude.

KAP. You think I'd ... For Christ's sake, she's married to Willow's father. It's not even decent.

ANDREW. I see. I see what you're saying. You're saying I'm not decent.

KAP. Don't start.

ANDREW. Because I am decent. Everyone knows that's my reputation. I've worked like a dog to help clear this family's name. I find it hard to believe you wouldn't know that.

KAP. No, because here's why, you're not decent. You're a sellout. Ed doesn't influence you, he owns you. Now the sweet part is you're fucking his wife. Plus you're married to his daughter which complicates your personal and professional allegiances to a point where it interests me.

ANDREW. Don't you insult me, because everyone knows you're the one who screws everyone. All the women. Every age, size and ethnic variety.

KAP. Not my stepmother-in-law! I'm not screwing her! I mean look what you're doing. People — Willow. She's expecting a kid and you do this to her. You do this?! People could be hurt.

ANDREW. Don't tell me, hurt. I've been hurt. You don't know how bad.

KAP. I don't want to know.

ANDREW. Because it was you — she gave me that letter. Willow gave me that letter.

KAP. What letter?

ANDREW. You know. Don't pretend you don't know. You know.

KAP. I know she wrote a letter. There was a letter. I don't know what it said.

ANDREW. Of course you know. You stole her from me. You stole her heart. That was hurt. That was hurt.

KAP. Look, we never ... nothing. There was nothing.

ANDREW. Yes, because she wanted to leave me. To be with "the one she loved." I know it was you. I'd stake my life.

KAP. We never even talked about anything. Nothing happened. Nothing was said. She's with you. She stayed with you.

ANDREW. It's not right. She doesn't love me and I can't stand her. The marriage is over. It's awful. There's nothing to do.

KAP. Leave her.

ANDREW. You'd like that, wouldn't you? Because it's what you've always wanted. You can't commit to anyone so you hunt everyone. Everyone's fair game! Even my wife!

KAP. Fuck you. *(Andrew shoves Kap.)*

LAFCAD. Stop! It's Mama's death day today!

KAP. I could take you. You know that?

ANDREW. I always best you. I always best you. Every time.

KAP. Not now.

LAFCAD. Mama hated it when you fought! She begged you, she pleaded!

ANDREW. *(To Kap.)* She babied you after. She loved you best.

KAP. Better than you.

ANDREW. She said you'd capture the world but all you've done is fuck and kill. *(Kap shoves Andrew.)*

LAFCAD. Can't you see our family has had enough?!

ANDREW. I just want our family to know and always remember, I am an honorable man.

KAP. I forgot it already. *(Andrew punches Kap. Kap punches him back. They fight. A low-down fight. Kap seems to be winning, not by much. Lafcad tries to break them apart, but he gets knocked in the shoulder and yells out. Kap turns to see if Lafcad is alright. Andrew goes after Kap full force. It gets ugly. Andrew throws Kap up on the butcher block among the mallard guts and feathers. He is strangling him almost to death. Lafcad gets a piece of wood and knocks Andrew off Kap. He knocks him once more and Andrew falls to the ground. Lafcad gasps, clutches his arm and collapses to the floor. All is quiet for a moment. Loud knocking at the door.)*

ED. *(Offstage.)* Kap, I'm here for you! I'm here. Open this door! *(Kap slowly gets up off the butcher block. He gasps for breath and wipes off mallard guts and feathers. Kap staggers toward the back door and goes out into the yard. He falls down on his knees and calls on his duck call. Demand, demand, demand. Ed comes around the side of the house and enters the backyard. He has been drinking.)* Kap.

KAP. Ed.

ED. What happened to you?

KAP. Nothing.

ED. You touch my wife? *(A pause.)* Tell me.

KAP. Ask her.

ED. I have to cut your face. A family tradition. I give you a mark. You want to fight? I'll fight.

KAP. I don't wanna fight.

ED. Alright. *(A pause. Ed takes out a knife. He comes toward Kap, who is on his knees. Ed cuts a deep mark into Kap's face. Kap falls to the ground.)* You mind if I use the facilities?

KAP. Go ahead. *(Ed goes in the back door of the cabin.)*

ED. I cut your brother.

ANDREW. What? *(Lafcad goes out the back door to Kap. Ed goes to the sink to wash blood off his knife. He stands there trembling.)*

ED. Don't say anything else about it. It's done.

ANDREW. Ed, I was the one. You should have cut me.

ED. She told me who it was. It was your brother.

ANDREW. It was me. Believe me.

ED. I do not. I never will.

ANDREW. It was me.

49

ED. I've cut all I can cut. *(Ed exits out the front door. Outside Lafcad holds Kap in his arms.)*

LAFCAD. Kap. Sugar. Oh, Kap.

KAP. I think it worked.

LAFCAD. What?

KAP. I was the decoy.

LAFCAD. Why? God, why?

KAP. I told Maude. I said I would. *(Andrew walks out the back door and comes into the yard.)*

ANDREW. I told him it was me. I told him.

KAP. Did he believe you?

ANDREW. No. No.

KAP. I didn't guess he would.

ANDREW. He should have cut me. It should have been my face.

KAP. It wasn't.

ANDREW. My face. Not yours.

KAP. It wasn't. *(Kap and Andrew stare at each other. They both know that Kap has won. Lights fade to black.)*

Scene 2

New Orleans. Cemetery. The Clay family tomb. The following spring. Easter Day. Noontime. Andrew enters with three large baskets of flowers. Ed follows; he is pushing Maude in a wheelchair. She is very ill. Willow appears behind them. She is eight months pregnant. They are all dressed up for Easter Day.

ANDREW. This way, this way. Here it is. *(Andrew stops at the Clay family above-ground tomb.)*

ED. *(To Andrew.)* You don't want to cut into the steak and lose the juices. Do it by touch. You touch the meat. Andrew, you're not listening to me. You're not watching. Come here, come here. Put down the flowers. *(Andrew puts down the flowers.)* Make a fist. Very soft. Now feel that with your fingers. That's rare. Tighten it: medium. Very tight: well done. You touch the meat.

ANDREW. Touch. Yes. From now on I'll know. Rare, medium,

well done.

ED. You don't want to cut the steak, lose the juices.

ANDREW. A dry steak can be dry. If you lose the juices. From now on I'll know. Now where should I put these Easter flowers for Mama? The orchids are for Mama.

MAUDE. Andrew.

ANDREW. Maude.

MAUDE. Put them there.

ANDREW. Yes. *(Andrew places the flowers.)* And for Daddy. The lilies are for my father. Aidan Oliver Clay. I still can't believe he's really here.

MAUDE. It can't be true.

ED. It was so unexpected. Intestinal necrosis.

ANDREW. It was the prison food. His intestines rebelled.

ED. We're all still in shock.

ANDREW. Daddy should have been here with us today putting Easter flowers on Mama's grave. Now I have two bouquets. Both of my parents are gone.

ED. It's a shame but we all have to die. Look around you.

MAUDE. Yes. I'd like another tablet.

ED. At your service. *(Ed gets her pills and water.)*

WILLOW. I'd like some water but I can't. Oh no, no. It's constant now. Trips to the little girls'.

ED. Andrew, have you given more thought to running for U.S. Congress?

WILLOW. I couldn't stand moving out of Louisiana. This is the perfect place for me to raise my children. I want to have a lot of children. Maybe a hundred.

ED. You're not a rabbit.

WILLOW. They'll give me something to think about.

ANDREW. My brothers usually come by to visit on Easter. Uncle Baites brings a picnic. We don't talk often. Daddy's funeral brought us together. I mean for the event. But everything is a strain. Lafcad berated me for not giving him the letter Daddy wrote for his rehearsal dinner. I brought it for him; it's here in my pocket. No one understands anyone. The truth is I'm tempted to run for Congress. You see, there are so many people in this state licking their chops hoping for my demise. I'd like to show them I have what it takes.

WILLOW. I'm not leaving Louisiana no matter what anyone does.

Andy, don't you care what I think? I'm having your child, that should mean something. Even if it doesn't, I'm not leaving Louisiana.

ANDREW. Please, don't then.

WILLOW. Let's go see my mother's grave. I'm getting tired.

ED. We all done here?

ANDREW. I suppose.

MAUDE. I think I'll stay here, if no one minds.

WILLOW. Let's go. Come on, Andrew. *(Andrew and Willow exit.)*

ED. Are you alright?

MAUDE. Fine.

ED. Thank you for putting up with my daughter. She's spoiled and rude. I'm really sick of her. I felt I had to see her because it was Easter.

MAUDE. I understand. It's fine.

ED. Andrew's responsible for her now. She's his albatross. I'll just be a minute. *(Ed exits. Maude takes out a lipstick tube. She applies lipstick to her lips as she looks out over the tombs. She feels the dead spirits. Kap enters with two long-stemmed roses. He has a scar on his face. Kap sees Maude and is shocked by her deathly appearance.)*

KAP. Maude.

MAUDE. Hello, Kap. *(Maude is sickened by the sight of Kap's scar.)*

KAP. Why are you here all alone?

MAUDE. I'm waiting for Ed. He went with Andrew and Willow to put Easter flowers on his first wife's grave.

KAP. Oh.

MAUDE. I felt bad I couldn't be at your father's funeral. I couldn't get out of bed that day. Please accept my sympathy.

KAP. Sure. *(A pause.)*

MAUDE. I'm glad to see you. I've needed to tell you, I'm sorry about your cut. I never should have involved you … So many years I loved Ed and he never … I was always second place. It was the humiliation. I can't stand that feeling and I lived it for so many years. He cut you and all that changed. What can I give you?

KAP. Nothing.

MAUDE. Good. That's all I have. How are the ducks?

KAP. Migrated, the bulk of them. Ducks are a very distinct, short season. It's not like golf. *(Lafcad enters. He is in a manic mode.)*

LAFCAD. Kap, you're here! Uncle Baites is coming … Maude.

MAUDE. Yes.

LAFCAD. My God, Kap cannot be seen with you! People are saying the most disgusting, torrid things about you both.

MAUDE. I'm waiting for my husband.

LAFCAD. Your husband! Oh God. Kap, go.

KAP. No.

LAFCAD. Please.

KAP. Don't.

LAFCAD. She's on our plot.

MAUDE. I'll roll over here.

LAFCAD. Yes, good. I'll assist you. *(Kap puts the roses down on his parents' tomb. Lafcad rolls Maude to another plot.)* I don't understand. Kap's name has been trampled through mud while your husband is viewed as some homespun hero. The man's a violent psychotic. Look what he did to Kap's face.

MAUDE. I saw.

LAFCAD. It's awful.

MAUDE. Yes. *(Lafcad returns to Kap.)*

LAFCAD. Kap, you won't believe who I found in Jackson Square painted silver, pretending to be a robot-angel with a false leg.

KAP. Georgia?

LAFCAD. She was so happy to see me. I gave her all the money I had. That's why I had no money for flowers. Where is she?! She promised me she'd take a cab with the money I gave. Uncle Baites must see her today. Georgia's rebirth on Easter Sunday. There's a significance there he would appreciate. Is that him coming? I see him. Oh no! I'd better go look for her. Don't tell him anything. I must be part of the whole fandango. *(Lafcad exits. Kap and Maude stare at each other from across the graves.)*

KAP. What do you know, Mrs. Chrystal?

MAUDE. Nothing, nothing, nothing! *(Baites enters with a picnic basket.)*

UNCLE BAITES. Kap. Happy Easter.

KAP. Happy Easter.

UNCLE BAITES. I've brought the picnic: fruit, pies, chicken! Picnics in the graveyard! A great New Orleans tradition. Why weep over the dead? We come, we go. We come, we go! My dear sister, Madeline. Mad-as-a-hatter, Madeline. And now Aidan has joined you. What must you think of that? Together forever in this tomb! Where's the whiskey? My spirits have flagged. *(Baites goes through the basket and brings out whiskey and cups.)* Kap, come here, sugar. *(Referring to Maude.)* Don't look, but who is that?

KAP. Maude Chrystal.

UNCLE BAITES. She looks terrible. *(A beat.)* Maude, happy Easter! Would you like to join us for a drink?

MAUDE. Only in spirit. I'm not drinking.

UNCLE BAITES. How do you stand it?

MAUDE. Morphine.

ED. *(Offstage.)* Maude! Sweetheart! *(Ed enters. He notes Baites and Kap.)* Well, here's a gathering.

KAP. Hello, Ed. Nice day. It's a nice day. Don't you think it is? I mean, Happy Easter! Happy Easter Sunday to y'all!

ED. Well. We have to go. Maude's tired. *(Ed goes to Maude.)*

MAUDE. What about Willow and Andrew?

ED. Willow's down there having a crying fit over her mother. Making a display. I left Andrew to deal with it.

MAUDE. How will they get home?

ED. Baites, could you give them a ride?

UNCLE BAITES. I invited Andrew to the picnic. In the spirit of something, I invited him. He said they couldn't come.

ED. Well. We can't be here. We're going home. *(To Maude.)* Are you ready, my love?

MAUDE. All ready. *(Ed starts to wheel Maude away.)* Goodbye. Happy Easter.

UNCLE BAITES. Happy Easter.

KAP. 'Bye. *(Maude and Ed exit.)*

UNCLE BAITES. We won't …

KAP. What?

UNCLE BAITES. We won't see her again. I feel it in my bones. A numb icy sensation.

KAP. Yeah.

UNCLE BAITES. He's such a horrible man, the husband. Why did you…? The cut? Was it for Andrew?

KAP. It was just something extremely stupid I did one day.

UNCLE BAITES. I've had those days. Let's drink.

KAP. Please. *(Baites holds up a fried chicken leg.)*

UNCLE BAITES. Chicken leg?

KAP. Yes! *(Kap takes the fried chicken leg and bites into it. Georgia enters. She is painted silver and costumed as an angel. Baites and Kap stare at her as she comes through the tombs toward them.)*

GEORGIA. Hi. Do you remember me?

UNCLE BAITES. My God. It's Georgia. Why, Georgia, are you real?

GEORGIA. I'm real. Do you forgive me? Can you ever?

UNCLE BAITES. For what?

GEORGIA. I lied to you. I was running away from home and I didn't want them to find me; so I changed my identity. *(A beat.)* Now I've changed it again. Do I look different?

UNCLE BAITES. You're silver. Silver.

GEORGIA. Yes, I perform at Jackson Square. I'm a silver-angel-robot mime. People put money in my halo. I make a good living. I eat beignets and drink café au lait at the Café Du Monde. I know it won't last forever but what if it could?

UNCLE BAITES. Join our picnic! Isn't this a miracle, Kap? The rebirth of Georgia as Silver on Easter Day. *(Andrew and Willow enter. Willow is leaning on Andrew, sobbing.)*

ANDREW. Come, come. Come, come. Please now, Willow.

WILLOW. The grief never stops; it never stops. How does anyone survive?

ANDREW. *(Noting everyone.)* Oh, hello. *(Georgia becomes completely still.)*

UNCLE BAITES. Andrew. Willow, dear.

WILLOW. Uncle Baites, do you have a Coke I could drink? I'm so weak and thirsty.

UNCLE BAITES. Of course. *(Referring to Georgia.)* Andrew, did you see who has returned?

ANDREW. I see.

GEORGIA. You can't arrest me. I have a permit to be an angel. You can't arrest me.

ANDREW. No, I wouldn't. That's all over. All my thoughts on that matter have ceased. Except to say I did nothing wrong. My intentions were good. I was completely faultless and in the right. Has anyone seen Ed and Maude?

UNCLE BAITES. They had to leave. *(Baites hands Willow a plastic cup with ice. He passes Georgia a chocolate bunny.)*

ANDREW. How do we get home?

KAP. I'll take you.

ANDREW. No, I'm sorry, but no. Uncle Baites, could you take us?

UNCLE BAITES. After the picnic. I know you said y'all couldn't come. However, you're welcome. *(Baites hands Willow a two-liter bottle of Coke and gives Andrew a cupcake.)*

ANDREW. No, no. Of course we'll come. We're here. I thought we had to be with the in-laws.

WILLOW. I wish you had canned Cokes. These large plastic bottles, I know, they cost less but the carbonation evaporates. There's no fizzle. The bubbles are flat.

UNCLE BAITES. Should I go get you a Coke in a can?

WILLOW. If it wouldn't be an inconvenience.

UNCLE BAITES. Certainly not.

ANDREW. Really, you don't have to.

WILLOW. He wants to do something for me. He can see I'm expecting a child and I have no mother. I have no mother to see my newborn child.

ANDREW. I'll go get it.

WILLOW. No, let him. He understands.

UNCLE BAITES. Really, I want to go. *(Baites exits. A silence.)*

WILLOW. Kap, why won't you tell us what happened to your face? *(Kap looks at Willow.)*

ANDREW. We need to leave.

WILLOW. Everybody has been talking about it. They are saying … terrible rumors I wouldn't repeat.

ANDREW. We'll get a cab.

WILLOW. My daddy's name was whispered and that woman, Maude. Isn't there a real story?

KAP. No.

ANDREW. Let's get a cab. Willow.

WILLOW. I'm waiting for my Coca-Cola.

GEORGIA. The plastic bottle has fizzle when you first open it. It's only later it goes flat. After it sits there open.

WILLOW. How do you know these things?

GEORGIA. Experience. *(Georgia takes the bottle of Coke and shakes it back and forth.)* Stand back! *(She opens the bottle, liquid sprays out. All react.)* See that fizzle?! There you go! *(Georgia pours Willow a drink and hands her the bottle. Lafcad enters. He is delighted to see Georgia.)*

LAFCAD. Well, she's here! You're here! Wait 'til Uncle Baites sees you!

GEORGIA. He has.

LAFCAD. Has he? When? Where is he?

GEORGIA. Off getting Willow a Coke.

LAFCAD. But she has this whole liter. I can't believe I missed the reunion. Damn. *(To Willow.)* Really, how much liquid must you consume?!

WILLOW. *(Crying.)* You used to like me! I don't understand why everything has changed.

LAFCAD. Because it has. It has. Don't cry. Why do you cry?! After all, our father is the one who has just died! Not yours! Yours is alive! Please, I'm sorry. Drink all you want. I'm sorry.

WILLOW. I'm thirsty, that's all! I happen to get thirsty! I'm dry, I'm parched! *(She drinks and drinks.)* Oh dear. I suddenly ... I have to ... *(To Georgia.)* Do you know where there's a ladies'?

GEORGIA. There's one over here.

WILLOW. Show me. Excuse us. Oh dear. *(Willow and Georgia exit. The three brothers are left together on stage. A beat.)*

ANDREW. You have to understand she's expecting a child.

LAFCAD. I apologized. I did. I tried.

ANDREW. It's fine. *(A beat.)* I brought flowers from us. Orchids for Mama. Lilies for Daddy. *(A silence.)*

LAFCAD. I can't believe Daddy died. All that time locked up. Never to be released except in a coffin. We're orphans now, you realize? We have no parents; no grandparents. Holidays will always be excruciating. I mean in a different way than before. And then, we'll die. We'll be shoveled into this tomb just as their bones are swept away.

ANDREW. I've been trying to hold our family together but I've failed. No one is capable. All along both of you have mocked me. I know y'all fed me a bug. Lafcad bragged that he didn't vote for me at the Cherokee Bar & Grill. *(To Kap.)* And you. Every time I look at you — there is the mark of my shame. You would think death would dwarf our differences. But it doesn't. It does not.

KAP. No.

LAFCAD. Did you find Daddy's letter to me?

ANDREW. It's here in this pocket.

LAFCAD. I'd like my letter. *(Andrew hands the letter to Lafcad.)* Ah, finally. *(Reading.)* "Dear Larry and Mary Anna, Tomorrow shall be your wedding day. A holy, sacred event. Treasure it, my dear ones. There is nothing more precious in this world than family. My dearest, darling, departed Madeline gave me three sons who are the light of my life. We have always, through thick and thin, been the ideal family. For us there has only been deep loyalty, happiness and truth. I wish you both the same. My only regret is that I cannot be with you tonight for dinner at Antoine's. Alas, I have been falsely convicted of committing a crime I did not commit. Let me take this opportunity to implore all of you at this dinner party to ignore the lies, rumors, and trumped-up evidence that has been waged against me. From heaven above my dancing Madeline looks down on all of us and whispers, 'My husband Aidan Oliver Clay is an honorable man. Exonerate him. Exonerate.' As ever. Daddy."

LAFCAD. Thank God you did not read that letter. I would have married Mary Anna. There would have been no choice. Our daddy.

KAP. That bastard.

ANDREW. Incapable man.

LAFCAD. We loved him so.

ANDREW. Yes.

KAP. Of course. *(Baites and Georgia enter. Baites has a can of Coke.)*

UNCLE BAITES. We're back! Lafcad, a miracle! It's Georgia.

LAFCAD. I know, I know. I discovered her. She was my surprise. I found her doing a show. It was marvelous; revolutionary! *(To Georgia.)* Show us your show!

ANDREW. I'm not sure this is the place.

LAFCAD. She's an angel! It is the place!

UNCLE BAITES. Please, do it.

LAFCAD. Go ahead.

ANDREW. Something brief.

UNCLE BAITES. Please.

GEORGIA. Alright. *(Georgia does a riveting mime of an angel learning to fly. At first she is very careful; she becomes more and more reckless building to a crescendo right before crashing. She lies still a moment before yearning for more. Lafcad and Kap applaud. Andrew looks around to see if anyone is watching. Baites starts to cry.)*

LAFCAD. Uncle Baites.

UNCLE BAITES. I miss my sister; I miss her.

ANDREW. Oh my.

LAFCAD. What can I do?

ANDREW. Uncle Baites. Uncle Baites.

WILLOW. *(Offstage.)* Andrew! Andrew! *(Willow enters.)* We have to go! My feet hurt!

ANDREW. All of you I have an announcement to make.

WILLOW. Are you listening to me? My feet are blistered.

ANDREW. Let's not fight. We're brothers, whatever that means, it must mean something. Maybe just that we are in the same family and have similar genetics or something more. It could mean something more. You only have one family and life is short. Shorter than we think because you never know when something might erupt. With Daddy it was his intestines. Mama was hit by a young girl learning to drive. Every day could be our last — that is a point we often overlook in looking to the future; so let us remember, not to fight. After all, life holds nothing if not surprises and we are here. We are here.

UNCLE BAITES.   Andrew, please, you must stop making this speech. I'm serious now.

ANDREW.   I don't mean to make a speech.

GEORGIA.   You are making a speech.

WILLOW.   Yes, you are. Now get me a cab.

ANDREW.   Fine. We'll go. I alone express my feelings. It's my fate. Goodbye. Thank you for the picnic, Uncle Baites. Happy Easter to all.

WILLOW.   Happy Easter.

UNCLE BAITES.   Thank you for coming by.

LAFCAD.   Goodbye.

KAP. 'Bye. *(Kap, Uncle Baites and Lafcad watch Andrew exit with his wife.)* My God. Leave me in a duck blind and let me sit there alone and still until night falls on all of it. For good on it all.

UNCLE BAITES.   *(Moving to the tomb.)* Beloved Madeline. Beloved, beloved.

LAFCAD.   *(To Georgia, tentative.)* Dance?

GEORGIA.   Dance.

LAFCAD.   Ah. *(Lafcad and Georgia begin to dance.)*

UNCLE BAITES.   My dear sister. Mad as a hatter, she was when she was here. *(Kap makes a duck call.)*

GEORGIA.   You're a good dancer.

LAFCAD.   I know. I'm lucky. My mama taught me how. *(Lafcad and Georgia continue to dance. Kap makes a duck call. Demand, beg, plead. The lights brighten a moment. Blackout.)*

End of Play

PROPERTY LIST

Drinks, glasses
Cigarettes, lighter
Sandwich
Cokes
Lipstick
Phone
Book
Cup of coffee
Plates of food
Potato gun
Bucket of crawfish
Notebook, pen
Cane
Ducks
Letter
Plate of crackers
Diamond ring
Mallards, knife
Bottles of scotch, liquor
Duck call
Cell phone
Wood
Arrow
Andiron
Ice
Washcloth
Duct tape
Knife
Large baskets of flowers
Pills, water
2 long-stemmed roses
Coke bottles, can
Picnic basket with whiskey, cups, fried chicken
Chocolate bunny
Cupcake
Letter

SOUND EFFECTS

Phone ringing
Thunder
Doorbell
Breaking glass
Rain
Explosion
Cell phone

NEW PLAYS

★ **RABBIT HOLE by David Lindsay-Abaire.** Winner of the 2007 Pulitzer Prize. Becca and Howie Corbett have everything a couple could want until a life-shattering accident turns their world upside down. "An intensely emotional examination of grief, laced with wit." –*Variety*. "A transcendent and deeply affecting new play." –*Entertainment Weekly*. "Painstakingly beautiful." –*BackStage*. [2M, 3W] ISBN: 978-0-8222-2154-8

★ **DOUBT, A Parable by John Patrick Shanley.** Winner of the 2005 Pulitzer Prize and Tony Award. Sister Aloysius, a Bronx school principal, takes matters into her own hands when she suspects the young Father Flynn of improper relations with one of the male students. "All the elements come invigoratingly together like clockwork." –*Variety*. "Passionate, exquisite, important, engrossing." –*NY Newsday*. [1M, 3W] ISBN: 978-0-8222-2219-4

★ **THE PILLOWMAN by Martin McDonagh.** In an unnamed totalitarian state, an author of horrific children's stories discovers that someone has been making his stories come true. "A blindingly bright black comedy." –*NY Times*. "McDonagh's least forgiving, bravest play." –*Variety*. "Thoroughly startling and genuinely intimidating." –*Chicago Tribune*. [4M, 5 bit parts (2M, 1W, 1 boy, 1 girl)] ISBN: 978-0-8222-2100-5

★ **GREY GARDENS book by Doug Wright, music by Scott Frankel, lyrics by Michael Korie.** The hilarious and heartbreaking story of Big Edie and Little Edie Bouvier Beale, the eccentric aunt and cousin of Jacqueline Kennedy Onassis, once bright names on the social register who became East Hampton's most notorious recluses. "An experience no passionate theatergoer should miss." –*NY Times*. "A unique and unmissable musical." –*Rolling Stone*. [4M, 3W, 2 girls] ISBN: 978-0-8222-2181-4

★ **THE LITTLE DOG LAUGHED by Douglas Carter Beane.** Mitchell Green could make it big as the hot new leading man in Hollywood if Diane, his agent, could just keep him in the closet. "Devastatingly funny." –*NY Times*. "An out-and-out delight." –*NY Daily News*. "Full of wit and wisdom." –*NY Post*. [2M, 2W] ISBN: 978-0-8222-2226-2

★ **SHINING CITY by Conor McPherson.** A guilt-ridden man reaches out to a therapist after seeing the ghost of his recently deceased wife. "Haunting, inspired and glorious." –*NY Times*. "Simply breathtaking and astonishing." –*Time Out*. "A thoughtful, artful, absorbing new drama." –*Star-Ledger*. [3M, 1W] ISBN: 978-0-8222-2187-6

DRAMATISTS PLAY SERVICE, INC.

DRAMATISTS PLAY SERVICE, INC.
440 Park Avenue South, New York, NY 10016 212-683-8960 Fax 212-213-1539
postmaster@dramatists.com www.dramatists.com